SEARCHING FOR TRUTH, JUSTICE, AND THE AMERICAN WAY: REFLECTIONS OF A WYOMING SURVIVOR

Other Books by Corbin Fowler

The "Logic" of U.S. Weapons' Policy (1987)
Morality for Moderns (1996)

Searching for Truth, Justice, and the American Way: Reflections of a Wyoming Survivor

by Corbin Fowler

© 2008 by Corbin Fowler
All Rights Reserved

Published in the United States of America by CWG Press

978-0-9788186-1-6

- Photos by Patti Fowler
- Cover by Chuck Gregory from an idea and photo by Patti Fowler
- Book Design by Chuck Gregory

Preface

This book is a collection of essays and letters written by me over the past decade. A few years ago, my wife Patti and several of my close friends, including Charlie and Judy Brice, encouraged me to publish my essays and letters. They were convinced that many people would enjoy reading the essays and especially the letters to the editor. Patti also felt having this book would be something our son would enjoy reading and having in the years to come, a reminder of what his dad stood for and stood up for.

There is no need to read this book in any particular order. Each of the sections stands alone. Feel free to start anywhere, and if one section leaves you unmoved, try another. I hope that at least some of these writings will be of interest to any open-minded reader.

I wish to thank Patti for all her encouragement about my putting this book together, and especially for her help in proof-reading and editing. I dedicate this book to my son, who even as a 15-year-old has a talent for writing and a gift for music.

CONTENTS

Preface	i
Introduction	1
Philosophy and Ultimate Issues	13
Religion, Morality, and Agnosticism	25
The Nature of Death and the Death System	59
Why We Should Not Torture	101
What's Wrong with Capital Punishment?	111
Searching for Democracy	127
On Our Own Again: Searching for Meaning	147
More Letters from the Earth: Selected letters to newspapers	167
About the Author	299

Introduction

Dick Cheney and I grew up in the "Wild West" of our country, and that could be the beginning of a tale of two very different journeys, but this is just my tale. I spent my childhood and formative years in Cheyenne, Wyoming—living (to use today's terms) in the heart of a "red State." My parents were both Republicans, and I took to heart the shining ideals and wonderful stories about America, The Beautiful. I was a good, young conservative (though hardly an angel) through my high school years. Indeed, I debated passionately in school for the 1964 GOP candidate for President, Senator Barry Goldwater from Arizona. For me the USA was truly the land of the free, home of the brave, the land committed to equality and justice for all, the champion of democracy and human rights around the world.

My journey as a thoughtful American has led me to a life of liberal patriotism. I have modeled my activism after scholars and literary activists like Albert Camus, Jean Paul Sartre, Bertrand Russell and Noam Chomsky. These are thinkers who followed Nietzsche's advice that we should "philosophize with a hammer." They shunned "ivory tower" scholarship in favor of coming to grips with problems of life and death significance for all of us. The old Athenian philosopher, Socrates, has also been a major inspiration in my life. Socrates believed that a citizen has a duty to be faithful to the good laws of a good State. He believed that ethics and honor must be the highest duties of a good citizen. His mission in life was to see to it that his fellow citizens, especially the VIPs and leaders, did not become lazy in their thinking and fall into corrupt and dishonorable habits. With this in mind, he said "An unexamined life is not worth living." He challenged the leaders of his society to justify their claims and actions, to prove that their actions were indeed examples of honorable living. Several times he openly defied the orders and practices of those who ruled Athens, arguing that their actions were not legal. Socrates' pursuit of his mission left his fellow Athenians deeply divided in their opinion of him. Many felt he was a great gift to Athens while many others felt he was a terrible nuisance and even subversive.

I am definitely not in the same league with Socrates' brilliant intellect or courage, but I have committed myself to a mission otherwise similar to the one he lived for 40 years of his adult life. I have for nearly 40 years questioned, challenged, and protested my country's authorities when I felt their policies or actions were unworthy, deceitful, reckless, illegal, or otherwise unethical. I have done the same with regard to powerful trends in public opinion and American popular culture. I have tried to do this on the basis of reasoned criticism and my evolving understanding of fairness and justice. I have followed the admonition of Plato who argued that the true philosopher must take the lonely journey away from mainstream culture to search for abstract wisdom. He argued that once the philosophical quest was completed, the philosopher must resist the strong temptation to simply enjoy his enlightened state without regard to his fellow human beings. He has the duty, Plato said, to return to his community in an effort to awaken and enlighten them about their misplaced values, to help them understand that they have confused what is less real with what is most real. The philosopher, he warned, will likely be rejected, ridiculed, and even despised for the effort, but he must try anyway. I have tried, acting as a kind of Paul Revere to warn my fellow Americans that they were asleep while the dangers of fear, extremism, and homegrown propaganda threatened liberty and justice both at home and abroad.

I never stopped loving the shining ideals of America, but the Vietnam War and going to college awakened me to the huge gap between the shining vision and the reality. I awakened from my dogmatic slumber (to use a phrase from the philosopher, Immanuel Kant), and the government I saw left me deeply angry and disillusioned. I realized that governmental policy, especially foreign policy, was driven by the "bottom-lines" of political power and money. Towards these ends, our leaders were willing to deceive and manipulate public opinion...for the sake of Empire and conservative ideology. The TV Superman of my youth had stood (Old Glory waving behind him) for truth, justice, and the American way, but those were not the ways of my government. It was not human rights and democracy that ruled their psyches, but unquestioned faith in capitalism and our right to determine the New World Order. Decades later, we would say, "New World Order, same old shit!"

The Vietnam War seemed to be endless, and the graves of Americans and Vietnamese became more and more numerous until eventually 58,000 U.S. military and 1,000,000 Vietnamese had been killed. We were told our sacred mission there was to contain the spread of Communism, to prevent one nation after another in Southeast Asia from becoming Communist, and to defend the freedom loving nation of South Vietnam against the Communist aggressors. We were told in 1964 that the North Vietnamese had attacked our destroyers (the Turner Joy and the Maddox) on the high seas without provocation. As many of us researched the facts and the history of our involvement there, a different story came into focus. Our ships had not been attacked in international waters, and they had not been attacked without provocation. Our ships had opened fire first, and there never was any clear evidence that the North Vietnamese patrol boats had fired any weapons in that infamous Gulf of Tonkin incident. This deception led President Johnson and our Congress to a major escalation of the war. It turned out that the government leaders in South Vietnam never were very freedom loving (except for their own personal freedom). They ruled South Vietnam with an iron fist.

It turned out that our government rejected holding democratic elections in Vietnam (as called for in the peace treaty signed by the Vietminh and France) in the early years of our involvement there. It did turn out that our government was committed to halting the spread of Communism, no matter what the peoples of other nations wanted. For the most part, however, the war in Vietnam rested on lies, deceptions, and delusions fostered by four successive Presidents, two Democratic and two Republican. The real game was Dominion over global affairs, and it was bipartisan imperialism[1]. As Henry Kissinger would put it in 1972 testifying before a Senate committee about the successful CIA led overthrow and murder of the democratically elected (Socialist) President of Chile: "This was a matter too important to be left up to the Chilean people." Many of us came to the conclusion that Kissinger might just a well have said "The United States is too important to be left to the people." The judgments of ordinary Americans just get in the way of international corporate strategy and the grand chess game of global politics played by our national leaders.

This was to be America's century, and only the Soviet Union and China stood in the way of unchallenged United States power in the world. Communist, socialist and leftist governments, as well as revolutionary movements, were the roadblock to the Pax Americana (world peace "American style"). They had to be turned back whether they flourished in Castro's Cuba, Allende's Chile, Ho Chi Minh's Vietnam, or Sandinista Nicaragua. As it happened, all this really had to wait until the collapse of the Soviet Union. The 21st Century would have to be the New American Century.

At home, the civil rights movement challenged the consciences of all Americans to rid our nation of the evil remnants of slavery. How could we be fighting for freedom and democracy around the world when we still had Jim Crow, segregation, and the Klan in full force at home? The images of the courage of young black youth and Martin Luther King, Jr. standing up (and sitting down) for an end to this American apartheid...moved many of us to see our nation in a different light. Our youthful idealism was challenged, if not shattered, by a series of assassinations and murders wrought against our heroes and fellow citizens. Not long after President Kennedy unilaterally halted our aboveground nuclear weapons testing and after having made comprises to avoid all-out nuclear war with the Soviets over Cuba, he was murdered in Dallas. The preponderance of evidence indicated the assassination was the work of a conspiracy, but all officialdom remained committed to dismissing this view. If only it were not so pitiful and tragic, this reaction by our Establishment might have been amusing. Surely, the one area of life where it is reasonable to presume that a conspiracy might be at work is where a powerful world leader is assassinated. I gather Julius Caesar's supporters would have thought it a dark joke if opponents argued they were paranoid to think Caesar's assassination was the work of a conspiracy. "Yes, all reason points to Brutus being a crazed, lone assassin," they might have said. "We must reassure our public that such conspiracies cannot happen in Rome." You can almost hear the Roman Senate chambers bursting with laughter.

Within a few short years, other leaders committed to peace with justice were assassinated: Martin Luther King, Jr., Robert Kennedy, and

Introduction

Malcolm X. King survived a decade of Southern jails and violence when fighting for blacks' civil rights, but when he expanded his Christian quest for peace and justice to attack the Vietnam War and to support the economic rights of Memphis garbage workers, he was felled by an assassin's bullet. Robert Kennedy was murdered after changing his stance on the Vietnam War and attacking the U.S. continued role as mistaken and immoral. After rejecting racism and the need to separate from white society, Malcolm X was murdered. Four students protesting the Vietnam War and the presence of armed Ohio National Guard on their campus at Kent State were murdered by a small group of the Guard in May of 1970. No one was ever found guilty of these murders. It really began to look hopeless, as if obedience or violence were the only values cherished by our government.

Awakened and disillusioned, my anger grew as I realized that the America I loved had been hijacked by the politics of power, greed, and public ignorance. I never gave up on the American dream, but I certainly despised those who continued to turn that dream into a nightmare of social injustice and warmongering. My love for the USA—my patriotism—was focused on traditional ideals of freedom, justice, and our Constitution. I believe our highest ideals must be protected against assault, and I saw (and still see) a grave threat to those ideals. It is not from foreign threats that I most fear an assault on our liberties and fair play, but from three homegrown sources: our government, growing fascist tendencies in our nation, and the overwhelming influence of big business on virtually every part of our lives.

Among many Americans, and certainly among our national leaders, there is an entrenched view that we Americans (of the USA variety) are entitled to special privilege and power in the world. Many feel it is our right to use as many of the world's resources as we find convenient to our lifestyle. "Our oil" often ends up underneath the land of other nations, but it is our oil. At least, it is our right to have open access to it and to have it at a fairly cheap price. Many also feel that it is our right, indeed our destiny, to be the Chief Judge and CEO of global politics. To this way of thinking, approaching a kind of secular religion, we are the beacon of hope and freedom to the rest of the world. When others in the world do not quite see it our way, when they actually oppose our foreign policy, they are usually viewed resentfully as backward, acting out of narrow self-interest, or even as the very enemies of freedom and decency. The formation of the United Nations was a good idea when our leaders thought it would do our bidding, but when it began to oppose and criticize U.S. policies, it began to look corrupt and irrelevant. The faith in American "exceptionalism" and Manifest Destiny is so strong that it often blinds our citizens to the reality of our foreign policy. Starting from the article of faith that America is uniquely blessed by God and that what is good for us must me good for the rest of the world, it is natural to see our leaders as nobly motivated and inspired by a sober view of the facts. It is natural to think that our missionaries of freedom and hope (often the Marines, the CIA, or Stealth bombers) must be allowed to spread our brand of capitalism and democracy to a needy and eager world. When our gospel or missionaries are rejected or opposed, many Americans naturally conclude there must be a misunderstanding or that the resistance must come from evildoers. How else could one interpret resistance to progress and salvation? After all, we saved the New World wilderness from the savages, and we then blessed the land with development and industrial progress. We saved Europe from Hitler, and we may yet save the rest of the world from each new Hitler. The world should be grateful, but alas sometimes the envy and ingratitude is overwhelming. Such thinking is, and has been, commonplace in our country.

Such attitudes strike me as arrogant and delusional, not to mention quite silly. Every Empire (from ancient Rome to the present effort to attain a Pax Americana) has felt itself to be "exceptional" and to have special dispensation from God or Destiny to rule the world. Every Empire has felt their gods or God was superior to those of other cultures, hence that the present Empire was destined to succeed where others had failed. Every Empire has become arrogant, over-extended itself (both militarily and politically), and thereby fallen as it imploded from within and was attacked by "barbarians." These "barbarians" attacked either because they could no longer take the abuse or because they simply wanted to replace the dying Empire with their own version of Empire.

If there is a loving and just God, I think God blesses no nation as so special that they are not constrained by the need for moral decency and humility. I think God would want people in all nations to treat Creation with respect, love their neighbors, and try to alleviate suffering. These sentiments seem to be at the core of the teachings of Buddha, Jesus, and Muhammad. On this score, there can be little doubt that the core values of the great religious traditions of the East and West, ancient and modern, are much closer to socialism than to capitalism. There seems to be no wisdom tradition whose spiritual ethics endorses the love of money, power, or even personal freedom.

My criticisms and protests have occasionally been viewed as unpatriotic, but I think only because some people mistakenly believe that strong criticism of our leaders (especially in wartime) is the same thing as hatred toward the USA. As I have written elsewhere, I love my country, but I often do not love the actions of its political leaders. Good patriotism depends on being able to make this distinction, for to do otherwise is to commit the secular sin of idolatry. What is great about our nation's ideals can never be sullied by the dishonorable or reckless behavior of our mortal leaders. To confuse our government leaders with the good of our nation is to affirm the cult of personality and fascism. This was cultivated successfully by the Nazi P-R machine in the horrors of Hitler's Germany, seducing a generation of otherwise decent citizens to march down a path to hell. Let us hope and pray that "America, the Beautiful" never follows a Pied Piper into the grips of such dictatorship.

Over the years, I have written many letters to the editor of local newspapers. Many of them are included in this book. In a general way, they were all designed to shine light on some or another problem confronting our country. They were intended to be informative criticisms of public policy issues and the ever-present dangers of ignorance and authoritarianism. Sometimes, I suggested my own "solutions," but often I simply pointed out what seemed to me to be threats to justice and democracy in our nation and around the world. A person can have the ability to spot a problem without necessarily knowing how to fix it.

I feel duty bound to point out threats to our citizenry, to speak out against demagoguery and other forms of tyranny posed by our government and extremism at home. I am proud to call myself a patriotic liberal. If any of my letters prove illuminating or any way helpful to defending our nation against neofascism, or to suggest paths to strengthen the seeds of democracy and social justice, I will be content that, through my letters, I have accomplished something worthwhile.

1. Read Daniel Ellsberg's *Secrets: A Memoir of Vietnam and The Pentagon Papers* (2002), John Stockwell's *In Search of Enemies* (1997), or Chalmers Johnson's *Blowback: The Costs and Consequences of American Empire* (2004).

Philosophy and Ultimate Issues

People wonder why some of us are committed to philosophy, especially since the nature of philosophy seems so vague and strange. I understand this wonder and perplexity. Philosophy is strange, abstract and distant from ordinary ways of thinking. One of my favorite philosophers (whose philosophy is very strange and abstract)—Plato—liked to define "philosophy" as the love of wisdom. I am fond of his definition for sentimental reasons, but I think it is misleading to define philosophy in such terms. I think almost all adults have a deep fondness for wisdom, but few are philosophers. Likewise, I think most academic subjects and professional disciplines have a deep regard for wisdom, but that does not turn English, History, Psychology, Medicine, etc. into philosophy.

Philosophy is a commitment to critical thinking aimed at clarifying, explaining, or justifying certain perspectives about meaning, truth, knowledge, ethics, life and death. I prefer to think of philosophy as an inquiry into the nature of truth and other values. Philosophers inquire where others fear to inquire or where they just wouldn't think of it. For example, is existence better than non-existence? Aside from Hamlet, Shakespeare's fictional character, few of us would ponder such a question. We take it for granted, unless we are feeling suicidal, that existence and survival is better than not being born or being dead. Philosophers do not take such basic issues for granted. Consider the following questions. Is it better to be moral than to be immoral or amoral? Why should we be moral? Again, most of us simply take it for granted that it is better to be moral and that we will be better off if we behave morally. Philosophers, on the other hand, can be quite eager to examine such issues and to see if our articles of faith can be justified. Doing philosophy is an unusual and radical undertaking.

Having an inquisitive mind and being ready to entertain strange questions is part and parcel of doing philosophy. But how exactly do philosophers do it? How do we go about philosophizing? Is there a method to our madness? Actually, there is, but there is enough diversity among philosophers to prevent a uniform, one size-fits-all method from being accepted by all philosophers. Philosophical method is more diverse than scientific method, and the reason for this is not because philosophers are inherently more rebellious than scientists. The issues philosophers address are simply more abstract and more ambiguous than the issues on which science focuses. These issues include subjects that are very significant to human beings, yet which are resistant to black and white answers. People with differing temperaments can reasonably adopt very different approaches to coping with these issues.

Let me give you two examples of my meaning here: one rather simple and the other more complex. Imagine that an earth tremor sets off a landslide in a remote valley. Imagine that rocks and rubble come tumbling down to the valley floor. Although there is no design to the rubble scattered about on the valley floor, neither is the result completely without order. What I mean is that we could pinpoint, say, each bit of scattered debris and locate it on a grid or geographical map. Having done so, it would become clear that there are limits to how any of us could view the "scatter-pattern." For example, beyond a certain boundary or circumference on the valley floor, no more debris would be found, so that any pattern of the debris itself could not be perceived to stretch outside of that rather helter-skelter boundary. Furthermore, of course, we have a rock and earth debris scatter-pattern (amorphous as it may be), not a sea-life, Scrabble game, or other kind of scatter. The landslide did not result in something extremely different in kind from the material on the sides of the valley walls from which it began. There is some order here, even if minimal for human purposes. Now, beginning from this minimal order, you can imagine people from different perspectives examining it carefully, yet interpreting it differently. Imagine a mathematician for example looking it over and wondering in awe at the beautiful geometrical shapes formed in the rubble. Imagine, on the other hand, a naturist poet looking it over and wondering in awe at the beautiful shapes of animals and plants formed by the rubble. One sees rectangles, circles and triangles while the other sees bears, deer, and trees. Both interpretations are reasonable and founded on the same order in the valley floor. No doubt there are many other possible interpretations, including the minimalist one I began with, and depending on which perspective you operate with, much more can be described, and different explanations are needed.

Let me offer a second example, a more abstract example of my point. How are we to understand the universe we live in, its size and origin? There is no doubt on any side that this universe is a vast, extremely complex, and often mind-boggling place. Now some are convinced that there must be Cosmic and unseen forces behind the existence and creation of this universe. Indeed, many are convinced there must be supernatural forces behind the existence of our awesome universe. From this standpoint, they would judge the adequacy of any particular efforts to explain the size and origin of the universe. Efforts to explain the universe in purely natural terms only would be viewed as highly suspect, if not downright misguided. Other people are convinced that it is only by natural explanations, explaining things by reference to observable and natural phenomena, that we humans are likely to explain any real thing. From this standpoint, going beyond the natural into metaphysical explanations is a sure-fire route into pure fantasy and superstition. In order to make sense of anything, especially Nature, they are convinced we must stick with natural explanations. Who is right in their approach? I think both may be viewed as reasonable ways—in general—to approach such a mind-boggling topic. Thinkers from both sides tend to view the other side as being fundamentally

Philosophy and Ultimate Issues 17

off base, starting from false or dubious assumptions. I doubt there is any way to demonstrate which side is correct or more reasonable, and in the meanwhile, both sides have a long history of developing sophisticated methods and theories to deal with the nature of the universe.

This having been said, there are some common threads to the madness of philosophers. There is a desire to delve into and clarify the nature of truth and other values. There is a desire to use careful interpretation and logical analysis to make intellectual progress. Philosophers examine the spoken and written word to evaluate the exact meaning and implications of what is being said, as well as to decide whether statements are factual and reasoning valid. Contrary to poetry which thrives on the rich ambiguity of words and metaphors, philosophy thrives on keeping different meanings straight, and (even though Plato or Nietzsche resort to poetry and story-telling to make their point) philosophers normally try to achieve clarity in communication and understanding.

Philosophers are also drawn together by a common tradition. Historically (at least in the Western world), philosophers have focused on certain abstract branches of inquiry. These include metaphysics, epistemology, ethics, and logic. Aristotle actually wrote a book called Metaphysics and another called Logic, so "our" history goes back to ancient Greek culture over two millennia ago—to Plato, Socrates, and the pre-Socratic thinkers. Metaphysics is the study of the most basic principles of reality, often with the implication that these principles somehow "underlie" the natural world we experience. If a person believes in God and the Creator or Sustainer of the natural universe, then this belief is a religious metaphysics. If a person believes that atoms, quarks and energy underlie every natural thing and process, then this belief is a scientific metaphysics. Human beings, though they may differ about "the details," seem naturally inclined to think that "behind" or "beneath" this world of complexity, there are more fundamental principles which, if known by us, will serve to simplify our understanding of reality.

Epistemology, also known as theory of knowledge, is the study of the nature and scope of knowledge. This branch of philosophical inquiry is directed at clarifying the difference between knowledge, mere opinion, and ignorance. How does the pretense to knowledge differ from real knowledge? What are the reliable sources of justified true belief: our five senses only, our ability to think and reason, a mixture of our senses and our thinking, etc?

Ethics is the study of the principles of moral right and wrong. What are the standards or proper criteria for making moral judgments, and how can we apply these to the real world? Must we rely on God's will, or are there secular moral standards that suffice? Is justice the moral bottom-line? What about duty, compassion, love, the greatest happiness for the greatest number of people? Ethics quickly leads to questions about politics and what is best for society.

Logic is the study of the principles of reliable inference or reasoning. What kind of evidence do

Philosophy and Ultimate Issues 19

we need to make our conclusions logical? How must our evidence be connected to our conclusions if the reasoning is valid or reliable?

Philosophers have taken two distinct paths over the course of Western history. Most have pursued careers of teaching and scholarship in colleges and universities. Here they study philosophical traditions and issues intensively in order to speak and write about their reflections to one another. This is the life of the academic community, a cloister for professional specialists who hope to make intellectual progress...and perhaps a name for themselves. Some philosophers (Socrates and Marx come to mind) become more interested in applying their insights beyond the hallowed halls of academia. They aim to communicate not primarily with other scholars, but with intelligent people in the general public. They are more interested in societal progress than in building new rungs on the ladder of academic knowledge. This split goes back as far as Plato and Aristotle in ancient Greece. Both these great thinkers had a deep appreciation for the joys of contemplation and of intellectual give-and-take with fellow philosophers, but each concluded that practical knowledge was more important than theoretical knowledge (although Aristotle seems to have been more ambivalent about this than Plato). Both wrote that the philosopher has an obligation to be engaged in his community, that the fruits of philosophical inquiry should be offered to the general public. Socrates is the clearest example of this commitment. He remained fully engaged with his society for most of his adult life, advocating a life of honor and humility to his fellow citizens. He served several times in the wartime infantry of Athens, and as an old man chose to die (as his sentence for being convicted of subversion) rather than abandon his belief that an unexamined life is not worth living.

In a very real sense, philosophers' involvement with ultimate issues is just a reflection of human culture's immersion in ultimate issues. While philosophical approaches to such issues tend to be far more abstract and radical than their communities are able or willing to accept, humans seem deeply drawn to ultimate issues. The clearest examples of this are religious doctrines. Whether we focus on the religions of indigenous peoples (hunter-gatherer cultures) or on those of more modern times, we always come across the conviction that there are ultimate Cosmic forces, usually directed by a God, which guide or control world destiny in one way or another. In a variety of ways, these extra-natural agencies are supposed to be "first" or ultimate in such a way that our own beginnings and endings depend upon our understanding them and upon our making the proper connections with them. Human beings, in general, seem quite unable to live without embracing "ultimates," and hence we can say that human beings are metaphysical animals. Even if there are individual exceptions, the rule remains that to be human is to be tempted by metaphysics.

One sort of ultimate question is: what in human existence is of most importance? What issues have most importance? Which is more important: thought or action?

These questions call on us to consider which items have more worth or weight. They call on us to make judgments of relative worth. After one considers Hamlet's question of whether it is better to be or not to be, and presuming one decides in favor of existence, one next needs to ponder what sort of existence is best. The radical French philosopher, Albert Camus, put it this way:

> *Judging whether life is or is not worth living amounts to answering the fundamental question of philosophy. All the rest—whether or not the world has three dimensions, whether the mind has nine or twelve categories—comes afterwards. These are games...If I ask myself how to judge that this question is more urgent than that, I reply that one judges by the actions it entails...Galileo, who held a scientific truth of great importance, abjured it with the greatest ease as soon as it endangered his life... That truth was not worth the stake. Whether or not the earth or the sun revolves around the other is a matter of profound indifference*[1].

Camus' view contrasts with the far more typical view among philosophers that people are too prone to act without thinking and that intellectuals are far better off to focus on issues which Camus would call "games." No doubt, part of the reason for this more conventional attitude among philosophers is the feeling that controversial issues, especially life and death issues, almost always involve intense passions, and these emotions get in the way of careful, objective thinking. The conventional philosophical wisdom may be summed-up as follows: better to be a careful, objective thinker about remote, academic issues than to risk the likely error to come from immersion in the passions of more pressing, concrete issues. Put otherwise, better to have your head stuck in the clouds that to have your feet stuck in quicksand.

Although I have some sympathy for the conventional attitude, my attitude is closer to Camus'. I think life itself calls on us to use our intellect to confront life's more pressing problems first, and later we can turn to the more remote and esoteric issues. For philosophers, this means turning our attention foremost to intellectual issues of life and death, justice and injustice, good and evil. We should use our intellectual powers to address mercy killing, suicide, capital punishment, abortion, religious faith and practice, social justice, animal rights, environmental ethics, and other serious issues. True, this involves the risk of subjectivity and error, but life is a risky proposition. We also take great risks by avoiding the great questions of existence on the basis that they are too difficult. In effect, this is intellectual denial. We stand to gain (and lose) far more by risking ourselves on life's knotty-gnarly problems than we stand to gain (or lose) by sticking to the safety of highly abstract theorizing about fluffy issues. It is a pitiful waste of intellectual abilities to retreat into the comforting isolation of our ivory towers. This is especially true in our present age when the problems confronting human societies worldwide are so complex and entrenched. We need the world's best-trained minds to apply their energies to helping analyze and resolve these life and death problems.

The essays contained in this work are my effort to come to grips with some of the more challenging, value controversies of our time. They are not exhaustive of all the great issues of our day, but they do cover some vital territory. As you will see, my reflections have a common thread: how to cope by seeking balance over extremism. I take it for granted (as did Aristotle) that the normal path to sanity, justice and compassion is the middle path, the path between the extremes of thought and passion. It is, of course, much easier to advocate this goal than to achieve it. I hope the reader will find that I have, at least in large measure, succeeded. For those who believe that extremism in the defense of virtue is no vice, my approach will be a hard pill to swallow.

1. Albert Camus, *The Myth of Sisyphus*, Vintage Books (1955), p. 3

Religion, Morality, and Why I Am Agnostic

People commonly associate morality with religion. This is not surprising, since all religions preach a moral code of one sort or another. In the West, we hear "Thou shall do this" and "Thou shall not do that." We are taught that joyous rewards await the righteous and hellish penalties await the unrighteous (or infidel) according to the will of God. We see to it that our children hear the same story. Since many religious teachings are unnatural in what they require of us (for example, "Love your enemy" and "Bless those who curse you"), moral commitment seems to require a belief in the supernatural. Accordingly, many folks think that we cannot be moral, or very deeply moral, unless we have religious faith to give us guidelines for living. It is very typical for people to think that God is the cornerstone of all moral value, and that if God did not exist, there would be no objective morality. In this spirit, atheistic philosophers like Jean Paul Sartre have argued that moral values are created rather than discovered by us. Christian thinkers, on the other hand, argue that since God is not dead, we should turn to God as the foundation for moral values.

What is inadequate about the rule or commandment-based ethics of various religions? To begin with, this view of morality requires religious faith, something which atheists and agnostics (like myself) do not have. Whether a person believes that God does not exist (the atheist) or that it is not clear whether God exists (the agnostic), he or she will have a moral code. Even if it is something simple like "Be honest and follow the Golden Rule" or "Be compassionate and be fair," the unbeliever will use the code as a guideline by which he or she hopes to live life and judge others' behavior. If a precondition of being moral is that a person must have faith in God, all atheists and agnostics are excluded from membership in the "moral community." They cannot make moral choices or behave morally because they are morally clueless, not recognizing their moral leader to be God. I think it is a serious mistake to treat atheists and agnostics as morally blind.

First, according to the Western religions of Judaism, Christianity and Islam, there is only one Creator, and we are all created in "his" image. Since it is ridiculous to interpret this article of faith as implying that we are like God in possessing heads, hands, feet or genitals, what can this "likeness" mean? I assume it refers, in part, to our having autonomous minds and wills, hence that believers, atheists and agnostics can use their independent judgment to discern the difference between good and evil, right and wrong. In other words, we are like God insofar as we have minds capable of independent thought and judgment. We are not robots or puppets. If I am right about this, then we are required, for example, to interpret the meaning of commandments like "Thou shall not kill." Does this mean that we should never kill, even in self-defense or to defend other innocent lives? Does it mean we should never kill any living thing? Some Bibles translate this commandment as "Thou shall not murder," and in that case, we must determine when acts of killing are unjustified, hence murders. I do not think it is hopeless to know the answers to such questions, and the faithful should have faith that God would not create us with the inability to find our way to such answers.

A similar issue of "interpretation" or judgment arises when we consider what we are to do in a situation where, no matter what is done, one of the Commandments will be violated. How are we to rank our priorities when religious commandments are in conflict with one another? For example, Christians and Jews have the Commandment "Honor your father and mother," but they also have the commandment "Thou shall not steal." What are children to do if their parents order them to steal something, which could be a special problem for some very poor and some very wealthy families? Jesus tell his disciples to "Love your neighbor as yourself," but how will this square with "Honor your mother and father" if parents tell their children to do things which are not loving towards neighbors? Jesus said that "Love your neighbor as yourself" and "Love God" encompass all the religious rules you need to know, but this means we must figure out how to interpret and apply them to real-life (often-complicated) situations.

Given the theology of Judaism, Christianity and Islam, it seems clear that human beings are endowed with the (God given) ability to think for themselves and decide what the right thing is to do. This includes deciding which is the lesser of evils confronting us. When we use our judgment to make such discriminations, we are using what the Roman Catholic thinker, Aquinas, called "the natural light" of reason. Thus, whether we are believers or unbelievers in God, this does not prevent us from having moral insight. Just because the atheist or agnostic has one blind spot (failure to acknowledge God) does not mean he or she is totally blind and has no moral knowledge. Indeed, except that the non-believer will, of course, not love God, they may be a moral "saint" in almost every other regard.

I am not denying that God, if God exists, would be supremely relevant as a guide to right action and the good life. God is typically supposed to be wholly loving and wise. Given God's perfect knowledge and love, God would always know what is right for us and would want us to do it. Given God's being all-powerful, God would no doubt succeed in communicating to us what is right and what is wrong. For these reasons, we would be wholly justified in heeding God's will for us; indeed, we would be very foolish to ignore God's will.

Ignoring God's will is one thing but knowing God's will is another matter. How can we be confident we know the will of God? Does God communicate this to each one of us directly? This is not the view of traditional Judaism, Christianity, or Islam. Each of these major religions maintains that God speaks to us primarily through select people called prophets (or Jesus for Christians). In the beginning God spoke to all of us directly in the

Garden of Eden, but since the fall from paradise, God chooses to speak to us through a few intermediaries (say, Moses, Isaiah, or Muhammad). Since these select intermediaries are all human, hence fallible, how can we be sure they got the message right? How can we be sure something was not lost in translation? This is especially a problem for Jews and Christians who base so much on the will of God they believe to be expressed in "The Bible." The problem is that the Bible was originally written by humans in ancient Greek and Hebrew, while contemporary Bibles are, of course, written in the various languages of today's countries. Is it likely that all the Bible translations over the past thousands of years have been wholly accurate in every important respect, given the fact that each of these Bible editions was translated by fallible human beings? We can see this problem surface in the fact that the original Hebrew translations of the Old Testament most often use the word 'elohim' rather than 'el' to refer to the divine, and 'elohim' signifies divine in the plural rather than the singular. We can also see this in the scholarly debate over a word used to describe Mary, the mother of Jesus. Standard translations have come down to us as 'virgin', but some scholars argue the Greek word originally used simply meant "young woman." Consider also the word 'angel' and what it means for modern folks. The Bible refers to "angels," but rather than meaning supernatural beings with wings, some scholars say it merely meant "messenger of God."

Beyond issues of the reliability of sacred text translations, there are other obstacles to our knowing the will of God. One is that different religious traditions claim to be well connected with God's will, yet they do not convey the same message through their differing sacred texts. For example, the Muslims' *Koran* states that a man may have up to four wives (provided he treats each one equally) while Judeo-Christian tradition has interpreted the sanction against adultery to forbid this absolutely. The Bible states that humans are supposed to master and subdue Nature while one translation[1] of the Taoist sacred text, *The Way and Its Power*, states that we need to befriend and harmonize with Nature. Which sacred text best expresses the will of God? Within the Christian tradition, we find that the Bible of Roman Catholics is substantially different than the Bible of Protestants. Catholics have six books[2] in their Bible which the Protestant Bibles do not. Does this mean that the Catholic Bible expresses more of God's will than Protestant Bibles, or does it mean that the Catholic Bibles contain excess "spiritual fat" while the Protestant Bibles have a more "lean spiritual diet?" I think only ignorance or a very stubborn attitude can keep people from realizing how difficult it is to know what exactly is God's will for us.

Is something right because God wills it? Consider the consequences. If something is right solely due to God's willing it so, then what if God willed that lying and cheating were generally good practices? If God willed this, then it would generally be right for us to deceive and cheat our neighbors. What if God willed that we kill all first-born children from red-haired parents? Would it then be morally right to kill such children?

Apparently so, if the will of God determines the rightness of things.

But, you say to yourself, such hypothetical circumstances are absurd. God would never will such awful deeds. I agree with you, but why would God not will such things? Surely, the answer is: because God is a perfectly good and wise Being. In other words, God's own character would prevent God from behaving in evil or foolish ways. God's own character prevents God from willing or doing wrong. This means that God wills us to do certain things (and avoid others) because it is right to do those things and because God *knows* it is right to do those things. Thus, God wants us to love our neighbors because God knows it right for us to love our neighbors.

On the other hand, I think it is presumptuous of the faithful to pass judgment upon what God would or would not will for us to do. If God has so far willed us to avoid adultery, this cannot guarantee that God will not have a change of mind about this. Who among the faithful is ready to say that God cannot or will not alter any of the Commandments? Surely, it is a great sin of pride to pronounce limitations on God's will (unless these are limitations based on what is logically possible). The faithful cannot argue that God would never will anything awful, much less what appears awful to us. The Bible informs us of God's having carried out or condoned quite a few awful acts against human beings and other creatures. Lot's wife was turned into a pillar of salt, land creatures were massively slaughtered in the flood of Noah's era, and God killed the first-born male children of all the Egyptians in order to make

Pharaoh let Moses' people go. Consider how God allowed Job to be harmed hideously by Satan or God's command to Abraham to kill his son Isaac. Thus, there is little reason to be confident that God would not decree terrible suffering, especially if one makes God's will the sole standard of right and wrong.

The issue here is not merely academic. Dangers exist in supposing that religion is essential to being moral. We are not splitting hairs to insist that the holy be separated from the ethical. It can happen when you think you have God on your side that you feel nothing should get in the way of enforcing your view of God's will. In other words, a person may confuse his/her own perspective and wisdom with that of God. This can lead to narrow-mindedness and intolerance, or self-righteous meddling in the private affairs of others. Such moralizing can become very harsh and can be hypocritical. Recall the Biblical story of the woman who was being stoned by self-righteous citizens for being an adulterer. Recall this admonition that only the person without sin should cast the first stone. Without denying the woman's sinful behavior, Jesus seems to have wanted the crowd to remember that such harsh punishment was best reserved to the pure judgment of God. But this purity of judgment was lacking in human beings. This lesson was apparently lost on the later Church when it so zealously sent out the Holy Inquisition to torture and kill so very many of its flock. So too was Jesus' teaching that we should love our enemies apparently not taken to heart by the Christian warriors of the Holy Crusades.

Religion need not involve a narrow-minded or intolerant approach to moral issues, and indeed the best in religious traditions usually counsels compassion and tolerance. Nevertheless, religion has shown a marked tendency to manifest its moral commitments in precisely such harsh directions. To the extent that people imagine morality must be the offshoot of religion, to that extent morality is at risk of being perverted into fanatical behavior.

The main danger here is that when people hold that God's will makes things right or wrong, this view encourages or reinforces authoritarianism and anti-rationalism. If the foundation of moral value is God's willfulness, then we should act "morally" for basically the same reason that we need to obey the will of a dictator—for fear of angering the dictator. Under the authoritarian conception of God and morality, God has the power, God made the rules, and God made the ballpark in which we must play. We are in no position to question God, and religious authorities often serve as the interpreters of God's will. So to question religious authorities becomes one and the same with questioning the will of God. This view winds up basing morality on power. Right and wrong are born of an act of Will, and the "moral" rules are legitimized and sustained by first the infinite power of God and second by the secular power of religious authorities. Right and wrong are not discovered by human beings through common sense and experience, but by select authorities or prophets to whom God communicates the rules to be followed. If we disobey these rules, we will be held accountable by the religious authorities and by God. Authoritarianism is based on the reverence and fear of power.

I have already mentioned an alternative way of conceiving of God's relation to moral right and wrong, a way which allows us to embrace a reverent view of God, yet avoid authoritarianism. On this alternative view, God wills that we behave in certain ways because God knows what is right and wrong, and being all-loving and just, wants what is best for us. God is worthy of being followed not because God is Super Dictator, but because God is benevolent and wise. This understanding of God does not make it necessary or convenient to exclude the atheist or agnostic from moral insight. The non-believer in God need only have faith in morality in order to have moral insight.

Finally, conceiving of ourselves as autonomous beings is crucial to any fully meaningful faith in Christianity, Islam, or Judaism. This independence is critically damaged if we are denied the ability to discern good from bad on our own. One blow would come to the integrity of the religious tradition which holds we have free will and are accountable for our choices (to follow God's will or to disobey it). How could we be accountable for defying God if we cannot tell the difference between good and evil? Perhaps even worse is the problem of how we are to know that it is better to follow God than to follow Satan. If we have no knowledge of good versus evil, we would have no basis for knowing that God is good and Satan is evil. We would have no moral responsibility for choosing God over Satan. The whole notion of human sinfulness as a moral issue becomes meaningless unless we suppose God allowed us to know the difference between good and evil. This means that we must have independent moral knowledge and that morality is not the exclusive possession of the religious. We must not only follow certain rules or commandments, but we must know which ones are good and which ones are bad. This, in turn, means that morality must involve something more than simply obeying rules or commandments.

Acceptance or rejection of the authoritarian model of morality has applications in other areas as well. Parents, teachers, supervisors, or employers may say, "Do it because I say so." Parents may say this out of frustration rather than really believing it. At bottom, they usually know that the reason their kids should do as they say is that the parents are more experienced and wiser than the kids are. The same goes for the underlying rationale for the good teacher. In other contexts, the underlying rationale can be less clear. With regard to politics, many citizens seem to think that government leaders know best even when the outward evidence points to the opposite conclusion. This disparity is rationalized by thinking that the leaders are in possession of information which the rest of us lack, a rationale often heard in the context of national security issues. The tremendous faith that such a conviction requires often borders on religious-like faith. Is it healthy, especially in a democracy, for citizens to adopt this authoritarian attitude? To me, it seems very dangerous. Even normally wise people can tell us to do very foolish things.

In the area of employee-employer relations, we can find examples of the submissive adherence to the authoritarian attitude. Some employees believe that the employer knows best to such an extent that they identify more with the employer's situation than they do with their own. Of course, if the employee, perhaps a manager, hopes one day to be an employer him/herself, it is easy to understand why they make this identification with the boss' values. Even if they don't hope to own a company, they may well hope to move up the managerial ladder, and the only way they can do this is to demonstrate their loyalty to the interests of their employer. In any event, consider the following real life case. At a Midwestern university, the Philosophy Department faculty were trying to decide whether to use graduate assistant funds to help create a new faculty position or to keep the number of graduate student assistantship positions at the same number. The idea was that by cutting one or two of the graduate assistant positions, enough money could be freed to fund a temporary faculty position. The philosophy graduate student assistants met to discuss strategy. Some students argued that they should strike in the fall term if the faculty reduced the number of assistant positions. On the other hand, one student spoke firmly against the strike, saying that the faculty knew best and should have the right to make such decisions. Another suggestion was that all assistants should commit a small portion of their assistantship checks to help subsidize at least one student for the coming year in case the faculty decided to make those cuts. The argument here was that not only was it a gesture of unselfish solidarity with the unfortunate one (who knew, after all, which student would be

Religion, Morality, and Agnosticism 37

cut), but a policy of self-interest since the student to be cut could be any one of them. It was also agreed that this plan would work only if the vote in favor was unanimous. The plan was put to a vote and defeated because one assistant voted against it. It was the student who had argued that the faculty knew best. Ironically, it was that very same student who lost his assistantship for the following year.

The extent to which people are willing to obey authority, even when doing so violates their conscience, has been studied extensively by Milgram and his associates. They found that nearly two-thirds of adults are willing to administer life-threatening pain to other adults, simply because they are told to do so by the authority figure of a scientist. In this study, the adults tested were required to give (what they falsely believed were) electrical shocks to other adults when the "learners" gave incorrect answers to quiz questions. Most adults continued to give shocks, even up to the 450 volt level, to the learner even though the learner screamed out in pain, begged for them to stop, and eventually stopped responding at all. Indeed, the "teachers" were told the learner had a heart problem. In the experiments, it was often very clear that the teachers did not want to continue hurting the learner and protested continuing with the experiment. Still, they continued after being prodded by the scientist or being assured by him that he would take full responsibility for any harm caused to the learner. Milgram was very disturbed by the experiment's results. If people would be willing to cause severe pain, or kill another person, against whom they had no bad feelings when told to do so by a scientist, what would they do when given orders by institutions or authorities with far greater power? Surely, we can draw one moral from this study. Obedience to authority can cause great moral evil.

Does being moral depend on religion? Does it depend on the will of God? Does it depend on the existence of God? Are we lost in a brutal state of Nature without religion to give us direction? I think not. Being moral is about affirming the value of others, of treating others in a respectful way, of believing that "I-Me-Mine" is not the highest norm. I suppose someone might think that it is only because God implanted in us a basic sense of right and wrong (which normally becomes clearer as we grow from child to adult) that we can have moral knowledge. Perhaps, but it seems impossible to prove that such a God exists (or existed), so this can only be a matter for faith or speculation.

Suppose you are Christian. Jesus says the two most important commandments are first to love God and second to love one's neighbor as oneself. An atheist can love his neighbor, so an atheist can be moral to that extent. Whether you are a theist or not, people know that no one is close to being perfectly moral, so the atheist cannot be denied moral knowledge or action simply because she or he fails to honor the first commandment. Furthermore, some atheists may be far better at loving their neighbor than some Christians, even though the Christians love God while the atheist does not. Similar reasoning applies to the perspective of Judaism or Islam. An atheist can hold in high esteem all of the commandments

Religion, Morality, and Agnosticism

(except love of God, of course) and hence can be very moral in that important sense.

People imagine that there would be no rock-solid foundation or no motivation for moral action if there were no perfect and eternal Being to certify morality, but this is an error. Being moral refers primarily to rejecting selfishness or narcissism as the basis for personal value, and an atheist or agnostic can affirm the value of being considerate of others and of rejecting narcissism simply on the basis of fairness and compassion. She or he may personally value compassion and see no reason why this should apply only to themselves and not to others. Their reasoning may also be as follows: "I wish to be treated fairly and compassionately, but what reason could justify advocating this only for me. Such an application would be arbitrary." Now it is true that if a person feels no compassion for others (if they are morally blind, sociopathic or psychopathic) or if she or he feels no compassion even for their own case—such a person will have no motivation for acting morally. But, of course, this will be true whether or not a perfect God exists and whether or not the rest of us know how God wants us to behave.

Now, one might think that only if God exists, can there be any objective and universal moral code (and any moral absolutes). But this inference rests upon the assumption that God creates moral right and wrong by His/Her will, and this assumption is questionable. If God exists, then either moral values are willed by God because they are right, or these values are right because God wills them. In other words, either moral values are willed by God because God—being perfectly wise and good—knows these values are best, or these values are simply created by the awesome triumph of God's willpower. If we assume moral values are simply created by God's willpower, then God becomes Super Dictator of the universe, and our motivation for following God's commandments is simply that God made the game and the rules. God does not know what is morally right or wrong; God makes it so, and if we do not follow the rules, God will punish us. This view of God emphasizes the absolute power of God and is a perfect match for humans with authoritarian personalities. "It's my way, or the highway" is their motto. These are religious soldiers who need only to be commanded and do not question why. Personally, I cannot believe in a God or religion who bases their values on Dictatorship.

The alternative is to think of God as commanding us to follow certain rules because God knows all moral facts and, being a loving God, desires that we do the right thing. Thus, God does not create moral values, but acknowledges them and urges us to do likewise. When God speaks to us, God knows what God is talking about and hence is worthy of being listened to. On this view, the religious person can obey God out of reverence and love—not out of fear of reprisals.

In any case, the fact that we can conceive of God in this way—knowing rather than creating what is morally right—shows that the existence of objective, universal morality does not depend on the will of God. Even if God did not exist, those moral facts acknowledged by God would still exist. Put otherwise, it is not God's will or human will in general that is required for the existence of moral value, but knowledge of certain values and the will to be compassionate rather than cruel or selfish.

As the current Dalai Lama, the spiritual leader of Tibetan Buddhism, says: "My religion is kindness." In this spirit, anyone can affirm morality simply by believing in the value of being kind and compassionate, by affirming being fair, and affirming that misbehavior should be corrected or punished...but in a merciful rather than a harsh and unforgiving way.

(My Agnosticism)

As a child being raised in the Episcopal Church, I had a fledgling belief in God, but as I grew toward puberty, my faith in God began to wane. I had no personal experience of God, and the Bible stories and Sunday school teachers left me with more questions than divine comfort. The church atmosphere seemed more like a funeral than a celebration, and the terrible music of the hymns left me cold. By the time I went to college, I was well on my way to being an atheist or agnostic.

Sometimes people think: "Look, you must either be a theist or an atheist; there is no other option." But, this isn't true, any more than one must choose to be hot or to be cold. You might well prefer to be warm instead. You might want to avoid the extremes. So that is how I find myself intellectually and emotionally. I do not believe that God exists, and I do not believe that God does not exist. I am not convinced by either view. I am like those people who are unconvinced that there is intelligent life elsewhere in the universe and who are unconvinced that there is no intelligent life elsewhere. Many of us just don't think there is enough evidence one way or the other.

Of course, it is harder to be objective about God. The idea of God is connected with the promise of being loved in an unconditional way, giving purpose to human lives, moral guidelines, and immortality for those who have the right attitude toward God. Believing in Santa Claus was very important to me as a boy, but I grew up and lost my faith in his existence. Actually, I not only don't believe in Santa, I believe that Santa Claus does not exist. Most adults have the same disbelief that I do. With the idea of God, matters are different. Believing in God is far more important to most adults than my childhood belief in Santa. In a certain way, the idea of God is the adult version of Santa, and most adults do not want to risk losing the gifts they hope to receive from God. Theists gain a sense of purpose or mission through their faith in God. Atheists gain a contrary sense of purpose or mission through their faith that God does not exist.

Who is more justified in this struggle for our hearts and minds? As an agnostic, of course, I do not think either extreme view is warranted. I think we are better off humbly admitting that we do not know whether there is or is not a God, and let it go at that. Few agree with me. In any case, when I talk of whose attitude is more justified, I am not talking about which view is more emotionally satisfying. (No doubt, for the theist, theism is more personally satisfying, and for the atheist, atheism is more personally satisfying.) I am talking about objective evidence and rational explanation.

Beginning with theism and atheism, the two extreme positions, which of the two is more favored by the available objective evidence?

In our time in our part of the world, when people affirm or deny the existence of God, they are normally referring to the God postulated by Judaism, Christianity, or Islam. This is a personal Being or Force which is eternal, all-powerful, all knowing, and wholly—the Creator of this universe. God is envisioned to be the Perfect Being, the greatest conceivable Being. Although I do not believe in any Transcendental God, I can think of God without imagining God to be Perfect. The ancient Greeks and Romans could imagine the divine without attributing perfection to the gods, and I think there is much to be said for an imperfect Deity. For one matter, it is simply easier to understand imperfection, making God less abstract to us. Furthermore, the relationship between an imperfect Deity and our imperfect world seems less enigmatic or objectionable. Still, let me focus on the standard Western idea of God, the Perfect Being.

What about theism? I do not believe God exists for a number of reasons. To begin with, I have never had an experience of God, nor any mystical experience that would make me more open to belief in the supernatural. Nor do I understand why God is not able or willing to make His/Her existence known in a fairly clear way to all of us, in such a way that only morons might deny God's existence. Furthermore, I do not understand why such a God would be so elitist towards His/Her Creation, so guarded that His/Her contacts with human beings are only with a very few, mostly long dead. I do think I understand, however, how a few persons can be deluded by circumstance and heredity. I also think I understand how many people can be, in turn, powerfully influenced (deluded) by charismatic individuals who promise them what their hearts desire: the conquest of death and vengeance against the unjust and all who believe differently than they do. Whatever delusions I suffer from, I have not been so influenced by any charismatic theist. I have been powerfully inspired by theists like Jesus, Moses, and Dr. Martin Luther King, but only by their strong commitments to the downtrodden, not by their faith in God.

I have examined a variety of arguments meant to prove the certain or probable existence of God, and I have found them all to be unsound or unpersuasive. For example, some argue that we observe design in almost every aspect of the world, hence that we should infer the existence of a Designer. This argument is very weak unless you already believe in God's existence to begin with. To begin with, even if it were sound, it could only show that there was, at one time, a Designer of the Cosmos, not that the Designer is still around. Secondly, I observe lots of order in the Cosmos (much less so at the atomic or sub-atomic level), but I fail to see how this order is indicative of Design. How do we distinguish between order-not-due-to design and order-due-to design? Unless we can do this, this proof has no legs to stand on. In any event, as Hume pointed out, the great diversity in the universe can just as well point to many designs (hence Designers) rather than one Design. The various arguments from alleged design seem to be weak evidence for *monotheists* to employ.

But if this is my stance, why not choose atheism rather than agnosticism? It is not because I fear taking a risk for something I believe in, but which I might prove to be wrong about. I have taken my share of risks in this life for ideas and values I believe in, and I agree that, for example, love and justice often require us to take chances where we do so because we *hope* our efforts will prove fruitful. I reject atheism not because I fear atheists are right, but because I fear their stance is too pretentious. I know of no atheistic argument that proves that God (whether perfect or imperfect) does not exist. Proving the non-existence of something is notoriously difficult—given our limited powers, our limited judgment, and the vastness of the universe. Proving the non-existence of highly metaphysical things is even more difficult, and this difficulty is only increased if one tries to do so with non-metaphysical methods and assumptions. Using common sense or empirical science to prove the non-existence of a divine being is like using a yardstick to measure the kindness of a good person. Yardsticks are wonderful for measuring many things, but are quite beside the point in measuring qualities like kindness.

A reasonable alternative to conclusive proof of God's non-existence would be an argument or evidence that shows it is unlikely that God exists. In other words, one could argue that given what we know, it is very unlikely that God exists. I am not at all clear on what probabilistic evidence for God's non-existence would be like, because God is thought to be such a unique entity/force. We, for example, are fairly familiar with what human beings are like, so we may reasonably infer that a particular person, say the man who never made a mistake in his 70 years of life, very probably does/ did not exist. We, after all, have an extensive knowledge base of human behavior, and knowing that the humans we know all have made mistakes, makes for a credible inductive inference that very likely no such person exists/existed. But our "knowledge base" about divine agencies is much less clear and much more controversial, so I am hesitant to say we can make reliable inductive inferences about God's existence.

Nevertheless, let us assume we can make probabilistic inferences about God's existence/lack thereof. Does the available evidence make it very likely that God does not exist?

I must say that when it comes to issues of such cosmic proportions, I doubt that any of us is wise enough to adequately assess the relevant evidence or the implications of that evidence. Indeed, it seems likely to me that the more complicated, vast, and metaphysical an issue is, the less likely it is that we will take into account all of the evidence needed to reasonably resolve the issue. Even if we leave grand metaphysical issues aside for the moment, consider how much trouble meteorologists have in accurately forecasting the weather 24 hours in advance, to say nothing of more extended forecasts. Shortly before the U.S. Presidential election in November 2000, most experts believed that the election would be close, but they were not prepared to predict that there would be a split between the popular vote and the

Religion, Morality, and Agnosticism 47

electoral vote for Gore and Bush, that Gore would win the popular vote, or that the outcome would be decided by the U.S. Supreme Court in a 5-4 vote The (non-metaphysical) variables were very complex. There were quite a few variables (the effect of the networks calling the election won by Gore early in the evening, the lack of uniform voting procedures in Florida, the importance of hanging chads and dimpled ballots, etc.) that could not be adequately taken into account. Doesn't the situation just get murkier all the way around when we consider complex issues that involve metaphysical variables? So it seems to me.

These "higher order" evidentiary issues aside, are there strong arguments to the effect that probably God does not exist? Whether God is supposed to be perfect or imperfect, does the available evidence point to God's probable non-existence? There may be arguments like this that I am not aware of, but the kind of arguments of which I am aware do not seem to work. The two I have in mind are based on the Origins-Explanation of the universe and the Argument from Evil.

(How to Account for The Origin of Our Universe)

Some atheists argue that the physicists' explanation of how the universe came into being is simply so much better than the hypothesis that God made it happen that it is reasonable to suppose that there is no God. According to the current scientific view, the universe was formed by a Big Bang that flowed from a mathematical construct they call "The Singularity." Prior to the

Big Bang, there was no Space or Time, but only The Singularity. After the Big Bang, a highly dense mass of matter was exploded in all directions—forming over billions of years, stars, planets, space-time, and other natural things.

Surely, this theory is mind-boggling and, I think, problematic. *Prior to* the Big Bang, it is claimed that neither space nor time existed. This is hard to fathom. If time is fundamentally a sequential change involving past-present-future moments, then it would certainly seem that prior to the Big Bang, the Singularity was $t-1$, and time existed before the Big Bang. For example, the implication is: Singularity at $t-1$, Big Bang at t, and exploding cosmic material at $t+1$. This appears to be incoherent if time is supposed to be created only at t or afterward. Also, this theory claims that before the Big Bang, only the Singularity existed, not a spatial world. But if so, the theory implies that the vast material cosmos of objects and events was created out of something that was not material or spatial. However we attempt to understand this, the "Singularity" would seem to be as metaphysical as anything postulated by Plato, Hegel, or any religious doctrine. Indeed, from the perspective of our ordinary experience, this scientific theory comes very close to suggesting that the material universe was created from a mathematical abstraction. This is not far from supposing that Something (vast) was created from Nothing (much).

Furthermore, it is quite rational to wonder what caused the Big Bang. Here science remains silent while religion, at least, offers us a Cause—an Eternal Being's will. In the final analysis, we are left with the question: which is more likely, that the universe was created from the Singularity (with no explanation being given about what precipitated the consequent Big Bang), or that God created this universe (perhaps by means of the Big Bang)? Both answers are problematic, but I think it remains true that the formation of this universe is consistent with the existence of God.

(The Argument from Evil)

This brings me to the other argument that atheists often offer why it is likely that there is no God: how can God's existence be reconciled with the extent and kind of evil we find in the world? Based on our human experience, one can reason as follows. The more a person is morally good, the more compassionate and just his/her attitude is, the more he/she will be inclined to do the right thing, including intervention to prevent or eliminate evil in the world. Now, God is supposed to be perfectly good, knowledgeable, and powerful, so if God exists, probably God will prevent or eliminate all evil that God has the power to prevent or eliminate. Since the more powerful and morally good a person is, the more evil he/she succeeds in eliminating or preventing, we should expect that God will be extremely successful at this task. But, there is, and always has been, an enormous amount of evil (innocent suffering) in the world, so probably God does not exist.

While I sympathize deeply with this reasoning, and there is little doubt that there is far too much needless suffering in the world, I think this perspective is based on some dubious assumptions. One tenuous assumption is that if God is all-powerful (and has the other perfect attributes), it must be within God's power to prevent or eliminate far more evil than God apparently does nullify. We can imagine this world without this much evil in it, and surely God, being all-powerful, could nullify that evil. What does it mean to say that God is "all-powerful?" It does not mean God can do anything, including the literally impossible, for that notion is incoherent. God cannot do what cannot be done. For God to be all-powerful simply means that God can do anything which can be done. For all we know, it may not be possible to eliminate all or most of the evil in the world because the effort to do this will only produce a greater evil. I do not argue that this is a fact, but it could be, and if it is, then it is mistaken to infer God's non-existence from the presence of so much evil in the world. In human experience, we know that sometimes the human effort to reduce evil in the world succeeds, and sometimes it does not. We also know that sometimes a sincere effort to reduce evil in the world has consequences that are themselves evil. The pervasive use of pesticides has made it possible to produce more food crops for people and livestock, reducing hunger in the world, but this same use has also made our foods more toxic while polluting water and ground sources. The pervasive use of anti-biotics has reduced human suffering and death, but it has also made for more resistant bacteria strains, perhaps creating an equally lethal threat for future generations. Other examples could be cited. We have positive evidence that good intentions and power can succeed in nullifying some evils while producing other evils. With this in mind, I think we cannot know whether God could nullify all or most of the evil in the world.

Another tenuous assumption made here is that God has not already succeeded in nullifying a great deal of evil in such an efficient way that we never know what we would have faced without God's benevolent intervention. How could we know this? What database for probable inferences could give us this knowledge? We can observe the evil which actually afflicts the world (hence, by hypothesis, which is not prevented by God), but we cannot observe evil which has been prevented from ever becoming actual.

Another dubious assumption made here is that God, being all-knowing, must know all the effects of any given situation, hence must know the future in a perfectly predictable way. In other words, our good intentions to nullify evil may well have unforeseen evil effects, but God is not limited in foresight as we humans are. It used to be hoped, even expected, that once we knew enough about the basic laws of the universe, we would be able to predict all the turns in the vast Clockwork which our universe was. In the 20th century, scientists have had to pull back from this view. One problem seems to be that the universe is vastly more complicated than was once thought, and it appears practically impossible to know all the relevant conditions well enough to make such consistently accurate predictions. Another problem concerns the exotic behavior of atomic and sub-atomic phenomena. At that level, it appears we can only predict *probable* patterns of behavior, and this less than deterministic fact may well be a feature of the micro-world rather than simply a problem of our human limitations. We cannot reasonably rule out that God, if God exists, created a universe in which many events or outcomes can only be known—in principle—with varying degrees of probability. If so, then even God may not always know when evil will occur and to what extent. As was already said for the notion of being all-powerful, we can say that God's being all-knowing does not mean God knows even what cannot be known, but only that God knows everything it is possible to know. (This perspective could shed some light on the story in *Genesis* where God holds Adam and Eve responsible for disobeying the command not to eat of the fruit of moral knowledge. If God did not know with certainty what choice they would make, God's stern reaction makes some sense.)

I think it is also problematic to assume, as some atheists may be tempted, that a Perfect Being could have created a world free of *all* evil. Of course, Western theists have tended to agree that God could create a perfect world, a Heaven beyond or a Heaven on Earth, so it is not surprising that atheists are willing to make this assumption. Suppose we contemplate a world in which people encounter no natural or moral evil except that which they inflict on themselves.

Perhaps this would mean that people never get sick, or very sick, and they never die unless they commit suicide. Suppose no one needed to worry about natural disasters and suffered only low-level anxiety. In such a world, it is reasonable to suppose that there would be so little to challenge us that we might become very bored. Indeed, boredom might become the greatest evil in such a world. After a person existed for several centuries, he/she might become very bored. Our present minor discomforts like minor toothaches, muscle aches, and boredom might then be considered intolerable and unjust major evils. Indeed, the only way people might die in such a world is by their own hands.

Is it clear morally and intellectually that God can and must create such a world—if God is perfect in love, power, and knowledge? Is it clear that since our world is not like this world of minimal suffering, probably God does not exist? I can only say that these conclusions are not obvious to me. Of course, many believers do think that God will create, or already has created, such an ideal world—a Heaven beyond or later here on Earth. Is it morally and intellectually clear that a perfect God would simply create that kind of world rather than first give us this very imperfect world? This is not clear to me. Indeed, we can rely here on our ordinary human experience for some probabilistic evidence to the contrary. Most of us seem to value happiness more when it comes after our having to struggle a bit, to overcome some obstacles, to achieve it. But this is the basic premise of much theology. It is assumed that God created this imperfect world as a kind of moral testing ground so that we could be challenged to develop our character and later receive the rewards of Heaven or nirvana. Of course, someone can argue that this world is much too filled with evil challenges, that a perfect God would have done better, but this again supposes we are wise enough to know how such a better world could be put together. I think the evidence is that human wisdom is substantially lacking on this score.

Consider some examples. People often imagine that once they are done with school, grown up, a legal adult, married (or divorced), a parent, have a steady job or career, become wealthy or famous... they will be happier than they were before. Unfortunately, it happens all-too-often that their inference is mistaken. Sometimes, when we achieve our gilded goals, it happens that we are actually unhappier than we were before. The reason for this is that we often get more (or less) than we bargained for—say, unemployment after graduating from school, drug addictions after we become "legal," a bad marriage, kids from hell, etc. In any case, it also happens that achieving a long dreamed about goal is followed by a let down; the contentment is not as great as we had imagined. People have imagined that scientific and technological progress would automatically bring about a far better, far happier world for we humans. Alas, very often the benefits of such progress have been accompanied by an unforeseen or underestimated downside. Car travel gave many humans a more convenient and sexier life, but it led to traffic jams, road rage, and great air pollution. Splitting the atom, many thought, would make wars unthinkable. They thought it would lead to a cheaper, safer source of energy. Alas, wars have not become unthinkable, even between nuclear power adversaries, and the radioactive waste created by fission nuclear power will be a lethal hazard to life for millennia to come. Furthermore, it seems that many technological advances have mainly benefited a minority of human beings (from the very wealthy societies) while threatening to end human civilization as we know it—due to ozone depletion, global warming, many kinds of pollution, etc.

I do not cite such cases because I am anti-technology or anti-science, nor because I predict nothing but gloom and doom for our future. I cite them only to remind us that we humans are fallible and that it happens fairly often that we are mistaken in thinking we know what will make the world better or happier. This being the case, I think we cannot safely assume that we know what God would need to do to bring about a heaven on Earth. The vaster a problem is that we attempt to solve, the more likely it is that we will overlook or underestimate some variable(s) crucial to our effort turning out as we hope. In other words, our record for getting things right *on our own* needs to be far better to justify our judgment about how God could make things better.

In conclusion, I find myself sympathetic to theists' longing for a God (perfect or otherwise) to provide various kinds of direction and comfort to our mortal existence. Indeed, I love the *idea of God*, and I am often sad that I am unable to believe that God exists. Nevertheless, I think the objective evidence for God's existence is fairly weak or ambiguous. I also find myself sympathetic to atheists' commitment to rationality and objective standards for belief. It can be dangerous to believe in entities whose existence is utterly beyond reason. Nevertheless, I think we are not smart enough, not wise enough, to conclude that there is no God. I see this intellectual struggle for our hearts and minds as one more example of human extremism. Some folks tend to underestimate human knowledge and wisdom, thinking we can know less than we really can. They are often led, therefore, to postulate a Super Parent to take responsibility for human existence. Others tend (no doubt often in response to the extreme horrors sanctioned by religious authorities in the past) to overestimate human knowledge and wisdom, pretending that we can know more than we really can. While I am tempted by both attitudes, in the end I find myself unable to accept the comfort of either. Both theists and atheists pretend to have more knowledge about God than I think any of us can.

1. Archie Bahm, *The Tao The Ching*, World Books, 1992
2. Baruch, Sirach, Judith, Tobit, 1st Maccabees, 2nd Maccabees.

The Nature of Death and the Death System

Plato wrote that the practice of philosophy ought really to be a preparation for death. Even if many students' experiences with philosophy classes tend to be deadly, Plato's view still seems quite morbid. On the other hand, if philosophy is about wisdom and if we care about wisdom, it is only proper to examine life and death issues. As a TV documentarian put it, death is the trip of a lifetime. For better or worse, we are all on this trip, even though we will come to the end of the line at different times. If we don't ask for some directions before we arrive, we may get lost along the way. This essay is an inquiry into the meaning of death: what is death like, and should we fear it?

It seems safe to assume that virtually every person in every culture has felt (or will feel) uneasy or fearful at the prospect of death. We know death is in our future and in the future of our loved ones, or we know that death has already separated us from friends and loved ones. Since death separates us from our loved ones (and perhaps a good deal more), death is a deeply personal issue for us. We also know that often death is preceded by great suffering or a long period of increasing enfeeblement, hence a loss of personal dignity. The taboos against suicide and the laws against murder are clear reflections of our view that death is a terrible loss if not a grand larceny. True, we normally are not living in fear of death (thank goodness for that), but this does not mean we do not fear death. Our true attitudes are only tested when we have to face something, and for most of our lives, death remains a distant eventuality or an event which strikes other people. When death strikes close to home or our own imminent death is obvious to us, then we discover our true feelings toward death. Given what we stand to lose, it would be astonishing if the prospect of death did not trouble us.

Death is a very personal issue, but it is also a very philosophical issue. No one has written about this more soberly than Plato. His contemporary, the elder Socrates, was Plato's inspiration for how we should understand the implications of death. For Plato, death was a guide about how to live wisely and honorably. Socrates died at the age of 70, executed by a jury of his peers for being a subversive. The formal charges were that Socrates taught atheism and corrupted the minds of young people, but Plato thought his hero's real "crime" was that he wounded powerful persons' inflated egos and stood up against their corruption. We must look to how Socrates behaved at his trial and execution in order to explore Plato's view of death.

At his trial Socrates acted as his own attorney, much to the consternation of his friends. He confronted his accusers in the same provocative way he had lived most of his life, reminding all present of the behavior that many found so annoying. He reminded them that for forty years, he had been on a divine mission – acting as a gadfly to keep his fellow Athenians from forgetting to live a life of honor and humility. The gods had informed him, said Socrates, that no person was wiser than he. This meant, he decided, that anyone was wise who, like Socrates, did not pretend to have knowledge (they really lacked). What revealed this interpretation to Socrates were his many discussions with the VIPs and "sages" of his community. In probing them to discover what they knew, he discovered they all pretended to know many things they did not. They were pompous and arrogant, and Socrates uncovered this fact in full public light. Powerful egos suffered wounded vanity and pride. Pretenders were exposed among elite groups within Athens, including various religious authorities, lawyers, poets, and politicians.

Socrates seems not to have taken his accusers' charges seriously, but he does offer a rebuttal. As proof of his sincerity about his divine mission, he reminds everyone there of his having lived a life of poverty for forty years. Furthermore, how can he believe in his divine mission (or in a supernatural voice which counsels him) unless he also believes in the gods? As for corrupting the young, he points out that the prosecution failed to produce a single witness to testify that Socrates had corrupted him (or his son).

He tells the jury that they must not expect him to play on their pity in order to win acquittal or avoid a death sentence. Only the facts of his case should be considered, nothing else. He reminds them of how disgraceful it is to bring in family members to weep and plead mercy for their relative (which he says some of them have done themselves when they were on trial for lesser crimes). He will not sink to such a level because he asserts that no person ought to fear anything, including death, more than being dishonorable.

This brings us to Socrates' doctrine of life and death. Many pretend that death is the worst evil, but he says it might be a great blessing. They do not know that death must be a great evil, and in any case, wrongdoing is the most fearful evil. Death, he argues, is one of two things: either an eternal sleep or passing on to the afterlife. If death is like the first alternative, Socrates says there is nothing fearful about it. If it is like the second possibility, he argues that the righteous person also has nothing to fear. In the afterlife, they will meet and hobnob with legendary dead heroes and even the gods. (The implication is that the unrighteous may well have something to fear in an afterlife.) Since Socrates believes in the gods and the paramount human duties to act honorably and be humble, he claims he cannot be intimidated into confessing to crimes he did not commit.

Following his conviction, he not only reiterates that the threat of death cannot alter his way of living, but he warns the jurors that they and Athens will suffer far more than he by sentencing him to death. He even goes so far as to propose that Athens give him a reward for his activities. Following his being given the death sentence, Socrates remains defiant and shows no sign of being disturbed by his pending execution.

While awaiting his execution in prison, Plato depicts Socrates as calm and resigned to his fate. Friends try to persuade him to escape, telling him that the authorities will allow it, but Socrates steadfastly refuses on the grounds that escaping would be dishonorable and would require him to accept one of two unacceptable conditions: that he change his ways or go into exile.

Socrates spends his final hours alive philosophizing with his friends about the nature of death and about proofs for our soul being immortal. Here he asserts that philosophy is just a preparation for death. As his execution draws near, some of his friends grow very upset, but Socrates remains calm and tries to console them about his death.

Having been given the poison to drink, he walks around a bit, apparently to hasten its effect on him. At his last breath, Socrates remains stoic and unafraid.

Socrates' death offers us a classic example of three familiar attitudes about death. First, death is (rationally) fearful only if you have lived a corrupt worldly existence. Second, for righteous, honorable or god-revering persons, death may even be a great blessing. In other words, it is sensible to fear the afterlife's punishments if you have lived a corrupt life. Likewise, the afterlife will bring rewards to honorable people. Third, it is ignorance to fear death because we don't know what it will be like.

Plato connects all this with the view that philosophy is a preparation for death. To have a proper attitude toward death means we must get our priorities in order. Death is inevitable for all of us, the righteous should not fear it, and the unrighteous should. To have the proper attitude and get our priorities straight is difficult given the many worldly distractions of life on Earth. Our bodily desires and five senses naturally incline us to materialistic pleasures of many sorts. This is a natural mistake. We are convinced that the most real world is the world of our five senses, the material world. But this is not true. The most real world is invisible and intangible. Contrary to the material world, the highest realities are unchanging and eternal – including our rational soul. Here there is eternal Truth, Justice, Goodness, and the Divine. But the only way we will be able to take this seriously is by a long exposure to and practice of philosophy. Only the abstract tools of philosophy can lead us, after long practice, to believe in the superior reality of eternal and non-material things. Without committing ourselves to this difficult study for many years, our body will — by its material nature — keep us convinced that the concrete world of our desires and sense perception is the very standard of reality. Because Socrates immersed himself in philosophy for forty years, he had no fear of death. His philosophical inquiry convinced him of the superior reality of eternal truths and thus made him eager to defend the life of honor and to depart this world for a better one. Death, he was convinced, was a doorway open, not a door slammed shut.

Plato's view is very intriguing and Socrates' calm and courageous death is very inspirational. Still, both are very unusual – hard for most of us to take to heart in our own lives. Few of us are as open to the abstractions of reason as Plato was, and few of us are as courageous as Socrates was. Our conclusions are not likely to be as definite or inspirational as those two geniuses of ancient

Athens.

Are we ignorant about what death will hold for us? Of course, we all know that (unless we are embalmed or frozen after death) our dead body will soon become ravaged by worms and bacteria, but are we ignorant of any continued conscious existence? Consider modern medicine's view of death. Here death is defined as the irreversible cessation of life functions. This understanding seems fairly straight forward, and it reflects many people's conviction that death is permanent. Still, I imagine old Socrates would not be much impressed by this view of modern medical science. I imagine he would begin his interrogation as follows.

> Do you say that death must be irreversible and permanent? If so, how did you discover this? We all grant that people die, but how do we know that people never return to life, or that a part of them (the soul) does not continue to exist apart from the dead body? To consider the first alternative, we know that sometimes people are pronounced dead and give every appearance of being dead, yet return to consciousness and to living. You would have us say here that although they appeared to be dead, they really were not. Why not say instead that they really died, but returned to life? If you say they must not have really been dead or else they could not continue to live, are you not begging the question and reasoning in a circle?

> Perhaps you imagine that death is the absolute negation of life as non-existence is of existence. From this premise, perhaps you conclude that

life cannot continue or restart after death, any more than existence can spring into existence from nothing. But do you know those premises to be true? Do you know that death is nothing and that death is the absolute negation of life? How did you discover this scientifically (or otherwise)? What if death is not the negation of life, but merely the opposite of birth? If so, then death may be a transition in life as birth is. Birth is the beginning of a new life separate-from-mother, but this doesn't mean that the unborn fetus was not alive. So too death could be the ending of an old life without implying that there is no more life to come.

Leaving the ghost of Socrates behind us, it is puzzling that medical science is content to define death as permanent. Even if a person is a non-believer in God or the supernatural, the many cases of "near death" experiences should provide reason for pause. In these cases, it is natural to say that people die, then return to life. In any event, what of cryonics and the hope for being revived in the future? A person is pronounced dead (head or whole body frozen in liquid nitrogen) so that if medicine ever learns how to cure or repair the condition which caused death, the person can be thawed out and brought back to life. I see nothing in this possible scenario which contradicts scientific theory or practice. It could happen. If it does, wouldn't it be odd to say of a person revived after 500 years that they had not really been dead, only near death? It would seem very strained and artificial to use this terminology. In such an amazing case, we should say the person was dead for 500 years and brought back to life by science and technology. If so, then continued life after death is a real possibility even if you reject supernaturalism.

Still, this strange scenario does raise other key questions about death, questions for the religious and non-religious alike. Even if our conscious life does continue after death, for how long does it continue? Plato wonders in the *Phaedo* whether the soul may exist only for a brief time independent of the body, then diffuse and scatter (perhaps like an early morning fog). Perhaps the soul and body are distinct as a tune played by the strings of a harp, the tune outlasting the plucking of the strings, but not for long. Near death or after-death experiences raise the same question. These experiences indicate that many of us will have continued, dream-like consciousness for some time after our vital signs are absent. In other words, in many cases our consciousness continues after doctors detect no pulse, breathing, reflexes, or brain activity, but for how long will this severely altered consciousness continue? Perhaps all that is required for some form of human awareness is continued electro-chemical activity within our brain cells. Once this electro-chemical activity deteriorates or ceases, it may well be that our experience also disintegrates. In any event, some continuation of our conscious life after biological death is a long way from personal immortality.

In her later years, Dr. Elisabeth Kubler-Ross, one of the world's experts on death, dying and grieving, became convinced that we all could look forward to life after death. Having spent much of her life taking a conventional scientific view of life and death, she later decided that there was a nonphysical realm which we passed into after death. Indeed, she became convinced of the reality of reincarnation based on mystical experiences she had and based on her study of near death experiences. One of the mystical experiences involved an extended experience talking with a former patient of hers who showed up at the hospital about 10 months after her death and burial. Also, she and a colleague collected over 20,000 cases of near death experiences from diverse cultures and parts of the Earth. They found that almost all of them reported very similar happenings in their near death encounters. Going down a dark tunnel or bridge toward a brilliant light or rainbow, feeling unconditionally loved as they got closer to the light source, and encountering dead loved ones were examples of what most reported. They concluded from this that these reports could not be construed as simply reporting the biases of their particular cultures or religions. In some of the sudden death cases, the people were totally blind, yet gave descriptions of their death scene, "minute details of the attire and clothing of all the people present, something a totally blind person, the victim of wishful thinking, would never be able to do."[1]

Another vital issue arises here. If we regain conscious life after death, will we be the same person we were before dying? It is known that sometimes people suffer strokes or are traumatized into a coma, and are afterwards substantially different in their personality when they regain consciousness. If such personality changes can occur prior to the trauma of death, it could well be that the same happens if we regain life after death. Surely, we might predict this for someone who is revived from a frozen state after centuries in cryonics netherworld. For some atheists, this possibility is an obstacle to their hopes of achieving a kind of immensely extended life, if not personal immortality, through science and technology.

This sort of issue could also be a problem for certain religious views of the afterlife. It shouldn't be much of a problem for those who hope for reincarnation since a person seems to lose his or her old identity each time a reincarnation occurs. Memory of the past lives are forgotten almost entirely and even if something about our soul remains the same across these many incarnations, it seems far-fetched to say that the same personality persists through these changes. Buddha himself argued that the soul's immortality throughout reincarnation should be likened to the flame of a candle which is passed from candle to candle over time. A continuity is established and in each case, a flame burns, but can we say that each flame (or lit candle) is the same? Buddha did not think so. In any event, our personal identity may be largely wed to our body so that getting a new body may mean getting a new personal identity.

For Christians or Muslims, this issue could also be a problem. Either they believe in the survival of the whole-embodied person, or they believe in the survival of the soul (or ethereal body) only. The bodily resurrection view (the first alternative above) faces questions similar to the medical restoration hope of some atheists. Will we be substantially the same person given the physical traumas we will have to undergo? The second alternative may also pose a problem for the religious perspective. If the body and soul (or ethereal body) are as distinct as they are imagined to be, then the association or disassociation of one with the other could well be a very traumatic event. (This seems to have been Plato's view.) One is immaterial and eternal while the other is material and destructible (the soul being thus able to survive the fate of the body). If the soul's becoming "detached" from the body is very traumatic, this metaphysical divorce could endanger the integrity of the personality, memory, etc. On balance, however, I doubt this possibility would much bother anyone who had enough faith to believe in God or the metaphysical relationship between soul and body. No doubt, such faith could leap these kinds of intellectual hurdles as if they weren't even there.

Considering the possibilities of what death may hold for us is enough to make a person dizzy and to reinforce the thought that we are indeed ignorant about death. Tom Nagel[2] has considered an argument that atheists in particular cannot imagine what their death will be like. The argument runs as follows. The atheist imagines that his or her death will be the utter annihilation of their conscious existence (forever afterwards). After death, they will have no consciousness, period. But, this they cannot positively imagine. To imagine something we have never experienced, we must turn to other experiences we have had, experiences which are similar in some way to the thing (state of affairs, event, etc.) we are trying to

Death and the Death System

imagine. But we have no experience which is similar at all to the utter absence of experience, and this absence is how the atheist defines 'death'. We can imagine something – even if it is very strange – but we cannot imagine nothing.

The believer and only the believer in an afterlife (so goes this reasoning) can imagine what death will (or may) be like. From this alleged fact, we can go on to draw some odd conclusions. One is that the atheist really cannot fear death since, according to atheism, no sense can be made out of the term 'death'. Even neurotic people paralyzed by phobias (of water, heights, crowds, enclosed spaces, etc.) are fearful of something, but the atheist has nothing to fear (except in moments when he or she wonders if perhaps there will be an afterlife).

Another odd conclusion (not considered by Nagel) might be drawn from the hypothesis that the atheist cannot imagine his or her own death, and it is even more startling. The conclusion is: I must be immortal. Why? Because if we cannot separate, even in thought, two properties, this is good reason for thinking they are necessarily associated with each other. Here the two properties would be my self and life. If I cannot even think of myself without also thinking myself to exist, it would seem reasonable to suppose I necessarily or eternally exist. Thus, we imagine that God is an eternally existent Being if God exists, that fire must be hot, that nine will always be more than eight, that triangles will always have three sides, etc. Of course, we also imagine that human beings are mortal, hence that they will die, so something is very wrong here. It would be even odder that atheists, of all people, should hold a view of death that implies they are immortal.

No doubt there are many ways to show why the above reasoning is fallacious, but I admire the way Nagel makes the point. He says there is a way in which atheists cannot imagine their own death and another way in which they can. When death occurs to a person, we know something about what happens even if we are not certain of the whole story. We know their behavior ceases, the body becomes stiff and dehydrated, followed within a day or so by the rapid bloating and deterioration of the body. We have seen it, read about it, or heard about it. We become "stiffs" as the slang puts it. Our lifeless corpse is a known consequence of our death. We can imagine this as we can imagine what we would be like if we were in a coma or in a dreamless stage of sleep. We can imagine people carrying our casket to the cemetery, speaking about us, or weeping over the loss. Imagining our death in this way is based on an outer or external perspective. It is based on what can be observed of a dead person (or their remains if you like).

Although much of our knowledge and imagination is based on observation of the world, we also know ourselves in another way – through feeling what something is like without observing it. Thus, we know how it feels to have an itch, be in pain, have a daydream or be happy. Take our knowledge of pain for example. We judge other people to be in pain by observing what happens to them and how they react. Seeing someone else get hit by a paddle and hearing them cry out are indicators they are in pain. This outward perspective is not how we know when we are in pain. We simply feel the pain without having to observe anything that happens to us. We know our own pain from an internal point of view; we experience it directly.

Now from this inner point of view, the atheist cannot imagine what his or her death will be like. They imagine that death will mean the end of any further consciousness or experience. They imagine that death will not feel like anything (much like being in a coma or being in dreamless sleep). Though the power of human imagination is vast indeed, it cannot stretch to cover the complete absence of experience. We are unable to feel what having-no-feeling would be like. Such talk is contradictory and incoherent. We might just as well try to imagine a rectangle which has only two sides. On the other hand, since believers in an afterlife envision a continuation of consciousness after death, they can imagine what their death may be like (going to heaven, hell, being reincarnated as a dog, etc.).

Has this discussion of death led us closer to grasping the nature of death? I'm afraid it doesn't carry us very near to the specific sort of answer we would like. We are left with the following either-or dilemma:

- **Either**, our continued conscious existence will involve going to a supernatural realm (heaven, hell, ghostville, etc.) or continued natural existence after reincarnation, divine resurrection, or medical restoration.
- In any lifetime, death is the opposite of birth (or perhaps conception), and it may be

the absolute negation of a life.
- Death arrives when our vital (physiological) signs vanish, and our body begins to rapidly disintegrate.
- At death, many of us will probably experience a dream-like state of consciousness.
- After dying, either we will have some sort of continued, conscious existence, or we will not.
- If some sort of conscious existence does continue, this existence may be ongoing forever, be ongoing for awhile (perhaps a rather brief period), be ongoing for a long time, but not forever, or not be ongoing, but continue again after some period of time (perhaps a very long time).
- If we do have continued conscious existence after dying, our personality and memories may be radically altered.
- **Or**, our conscious existence will in no way continue after dying, and death will mean the end of our personal existence forever.

These meager certainties don't take us very far. The various possibilities are very diverse in a way that is not comforting. Indeed, for those who reject spiritual or supernatural explanations of death, there is one probability that could leave them unsettled. Suppose their last conscious experiences will be the nightmarish variety that some report who have had "near-death" experiences. Even supposing that these experiences don't last long in clock time or objective time, their experience at that point will be immersed in the subjective time of dream-states. They will have no way to reassure themselves in those fragmented moments that the experience will not last long. They will have no objective standard with which to place their hellish experiences in perspective. Thus, a few minutes will, no doubt, seem like an eternity. Subjective time does not fly when you are not having fun. This will likely not be much comfort to atheists and agnostics.

This brings us to another key issue about the nature of death: is death worthy of fear or dread? For the religious person, the reasonable answer can easily be yes. If we will somehow pass on to another realm of existence, and this may be hell or a ghost-like existence, then people may rationally fear that this will happen to them. The prospect of being eternally tortured is very fearful, and dread is also quite appropriate for the usual depiction of the cold and forlorn state of ghosts. Not being completely sure that you will go to heaven (and who can be?) is an uncertainty which can lead to some sleepless nights.

Similar anxiety (though likely not as extreme) can be experienced if you believe in reincarnation. Perhaps, in your next incarnation, your accumulated karmic debt will be great enough to place you in a fairly miserable existence. What, for example, if you are reincarnated as a quadriplegic or as a cockroach? Such prospects could make a person feel very uneasy about death.

One thinker has argued that the case is very different for the thoroughgoing atheist. Tom Nagel[3] has claimed that it is really very odd for such a person to fear death. To begin with, he says they do not have to fret about going to hell since they don't believe in such things. So, what is it about death that could scare them? Apparently, it is the finality of death for them as they imagine it. Death will mean the end of their life and consciousness forever afterwards. Unless they are immortalists (who place their fate in the hands of cryonics and future medicine), this is the attitude atheists have toward their own death.

But, says Nagel, on their own view, there is nothing for them to fear. It is not going to be something positive and evil which one day will assault their experience. It will not be an experience of pain, torment, humiliation, depression, or even boredom. Death will be, so atheists think, the absolute annihilation of their consciousness. Their worries will be over. They will have no more experiences of anything negative. Perhaps, atheists could be anxious about their death because they do not want their life to be discontinued, but how can this blossom into fear? Nagel does not doubt that there are atheists who fear their own death, but he suspects such fear is irrational: a phobia or paranoia. For example, to fear being around particular groups of people because they have been cruel to you before is a rationally founded fear. To be fearful around other people no matter who they are would be an extreme agoraphobia, an irrational fear.

Is Nagel right about this? Must an atheist who fears death be considered irrational in their attitude? I don't think so. As atheists conceive of death, they not only will cease having any negative experiences, but they also will cease to have any positively good ones either. No more anxiety, but no more satisfaction either. In general, it is rational to fear losing everything good in your life. In general, it is rational to fear losing control over your life. Death, as atheists imagine it, is the ultimate thief. On their view, death robs us absolutely of our liberty and any further potential for happiness. Never again to go for a walk, have a good dinner, play with a friend, embrace a loved one; this is what death implies for the atheist. Death pulls the rug out from underneath their feet. How could a person not feel deeply troubled by the prospect of losing all control over their life? I think it would be odd if a person didn't fear such a state of affairs.

Though Nagel doesn't say so, someone might say: "To spit against the wind is foolish. Since our death is unavoidable, we are sensible to accept this, not to fear it." While I agree it is best to resign yourself to your ultimate demise, and not to pretend you are a god, I still think it is understandable and reasonable for an atheist to fear death. First, the very fact that an evil is unavoidable does not diminish that evil; indeed, I would think its inevitability increases the anxiety or fear we are likely to feel toward it. We should feel less fearful toward some evil if we have it in our power to avoid it. For example, because of fantastic advances in pain management, going to the dentist is immensely less fearful than it used to be. Second, if we do have a powerful instinct (or drive) to survive and most of our societal teaching is aimed at reinforcing the value of survival, it is hardly odd if we feel deeply disturbed by the inevitability of our failure. At least, the religious have hope that their life (in some way) will continue after death. For the atheist, this hope is truly unreasonable. For the atheist, death can reasonably be viewed as the ultimate underminer of hope. If anyone has good reason to fear death, the atheist does.

I don't mean to say that the wisest course is for the atheist to remain mired in fear of death. Fear is destructive of personal happiness and dignity, and thus there is the saying that the only thing we have to fear is fear itself. Having acknowledged one's fear of death, the atheist would be wise to seek ways to overcome or diminish this fear. On this score, practicing meditation and studying Buddhism, especially Zen Buddhism or Taoism, could be very helpful to the atheist. Buddhism and Taoism teach psychophysical exercises whose practice offers the reasonable hope of diminishing our anxiety about any present or future evil. These practices work by focusing our mind on the present moment and letting go of our urge to be in control of everything. Meditation has even proved successful in diminishing the agony of some who suffer from chronic and severe pain. Better still for the atheist, the doctrines of Zen and Taoism can be interpreted in very naturalistic ways.

Whether you believe in some sort of after-life or you think that this lifetime is the only one we get, it is very understandable if you feel anxious or fearful toward death. Whether death means to you the chance that you will suffer greatly in a continued existence or it means for you the final end to any further happiness, the thought of death can be deeply troubling. Add to this the possibility that your view of death is mistaken, and more anxiety can set in. For example, you may make certain sacrifices in your life in the belief this must be done as a preparation for the afterlife. If there will be no afterlife, your sacrifices may be in vain. On the other hand, as an atheist, you may discover that there is an afterlife in which you will be punished for your lack of faith. There is enough uncertainty about the nature of death to make anyone fearful about their prospects.

Morbid or sad as the thought may be, life depends on death. Life cannot go on without killing. This is not a warm and fuzzy idea, but it is true. One organism attacks and kills another in order to survive. Killing to sustain life is a normal feature of Nature at all levels. Larger creatures kill smaller ones, smaller ones kill larger ones, and "equals kill equals." As we move about, eat, drink and breathe, we kill great numbers of smaller creatures: insects and bacteria. Our digestive and immune systems function as an assault force against microbes that enter our bodies. All-too-often these microbes defeat our bodily immune system, causing illness and death. If nothing died, you might think that overcrowding and stagnation would be the major problem, but think again. If nothing died, what would we eat? How would the soil's fertility be maintained without dead leaves and other organisms providing the fertilizer? Without death, life itself seems impossible.

To protect and preserve life is the function of the death system. At the human level, there are three components of the death system: physiological, psychological, and institutional. The physiological component includes pain and our bodily immune system. When we are injured or ill, we normally feel pain. Pain is a warning, a red flag, that we have a problem. It is our bodily early warning system. If we did not experience pain or discomfort, the quality of our life would be severely damaged, and we would not live very long. Having no pain sensations, problems would go untreated and only grow worse. (This does not mean that we should feel good about pain, or that severe pain should go untreated.) Physical pain and discomfort are necessary elements of life. The attack cells, which constitute our immune system, preserve our health and our life by being efficient killers of foreign invaders. When our bodily immune system is weakened or neutralized (for example, by radiation exposure or the HIV virus), we get sick or die.

The psychological component of our death system includes denial, grieving, and emotional pain. Our natural tendency to deny (ignore, minimize or suppress) painful or threatening experiences is a double-edged sword. On the one hand, it is vital for our sanity and survival. If we always were aware of every painful or frightening experience we have had or might have, our nerves would be shot. Our emotional circuits would be overloaded by trauma. We would suffer from shock, acute depression or fear, and likely be paranoid. Such an overload would cause us to short circuit, to have a nervous breakdown, and be thoroughly miserable. In such a state, we could not function rationally and hence not be able to cope with the world. In this sense, some substantial degree of denial is essential to our life. On the other hand, if we sink too far into denial, we also become severe threats to our life and other life. By refusing to acknowledge real threats to our life (and other life), we live in a fantasy world that makes us reckless. For example, if I am totally fearless, then I will take risks that endanger my life and other lives. If I am a world leader who has control over the use of nuclear weapons and I have no fear of nuclear war, heaven help the rest of us. If I fear death too much, I will be paralyzed by fear. If I fear death too little, I will be emboldened to take risks that bring death nearer to myself and those who are affected by my rash actions. Finding a happy medium between these extreme attitudes is not always easy, but it is necessary for protecting life.

The process of grieving for the death of someone we love is another component of the death system's psychology. When we are confronted with the loss, or the impending loss, of someone we love, we naturally react to defend ourselves, to heal the emotional wound. This process is paralleled in the way our body normally reacts to an injury or illness. Normally, we feel some pain or discomfort (which may come and go for awhile) as our body attempts to heal itself. The process may be messy and interfere with our normal functioning, but it is a necessary part of the healing process. Think of grieving over a beloved's death as somewhat like being cut. A scab forms and eventually falls off. Emotionally, grief over the death of a loved one is a response to an acute injury. We must expect severe or prolonged discomfort when we lose anything or anyone we love.

Mental health experts[4] say the process of bereavement typically involves the following stages: denial, anger or fear, bargaining, depression, acceptance. We don't always experience all of these, and we don't necessarily experience them in this order, but the bereaved can expect to experience most or all of these attitudes.

The psychology of grieving concerns a more general and yet very personal truth. From birth (or conception) we all face a terminal condition; we are all under a death sentence. The death system includes the function of consoling and comforting us. As we go through life, we are increasingly confronted with the fact of death: death of relationships, of certain feelings, of strangers, family members, friends, and the death of other living things. We receive more and more reminders of our own mortality. Since nearly all of us find this prospect depressing (if not terrible), it is natural for us to engage in a lot of rationalizing (the close ally of denial). The older we are, the fewer of our family and friends remain alive. The misfortunes of traffic and plane fatalities, epidemics like AIDS, war and terrorism, Chernobyl, and natural disasters (to mention a few) serve as reminders of our own impending death. To escape these morbid reminders, we tend to think our way past our own death sentence. We erect mental barricades to protect us from having to take our own death too seriously. If we are young, we think of death as something that happens to old people. If we are a smoker, we think of death-by-cancer statistically. "Okay, it befalls lots of smokers, but not all, and many don't ever get cancer." We think of death as a misfortune that befalls the other guy or gal, people who are not as lucky or healthy as we are. As we grow old, we think of ourselves as growing older (not old), which as George Carlin says, makes it seem like a process that will take longer. Some even hope to conquer death by doing death-defying feats (perhaps car racing, sky diving, or mountain climbing). Here the logic seems to be: if I only confront and challenge death, it cannot sneak up on me and take me "unawares." Others hope to defeat death through the technology of cryonics – allowing them to hope for a kind of physical immortality which transcends religious faith. Often we bury our fear of death in pain-concealing language. Thus, we speak of people "passing away" (how lucky they did not die!), of someone being eighty years "young," of nuclear "devices" (not bombs), of "collateral damage" (not civilian casualties) from bombing missions, or of a "pre-emptive strategic countervalue strike" rather than a first use of hydrogen bombs on civilian targets.

How do we rationalize such eerie behavior? By thinking that death is inevitable, so why fret about it? By saying we might as well put a happy face on an unpleasant and unavoidable reality? By saying where there's life, there is hope? By thinking that national security requires dreadful preparations, and we would be less likely to face up to these dreadful obligations if we candidly spoke of their horrible consequences? But no matter how we rationalize it and no matter what good reasons we may have for doing so, the fact remains that it is hard for us to accept our own death (and the death of those we love). As a result, we delude ourselves in a myriad of ways. Our ability to rationalize the power that death holds over us is a major consolation to us in a battle we are bound to lose. Nevertheless, to the extent that this allows us to deny the reality of death, to that extent we may be inviting the reckless or careless behavior that will actually bring death closer to us all.

The final component of the death system is institutional. This refers us to many rituals, customs, businesses, government agencies, and public policy decisions. All of the following play a role here: churches, hospitals, hospices, funeral homes, cemeteries, life (death) insurance, last will and testaments, the food industry, police, capital punishment, armed forces, national security agencies, war, etc. Huge sectors of our society are devoted to preparing for death or killing. The food industry depends upon mass slaughter of animals and plants to feed a large and growing population. Other industries are devoted to disposing of dead bodies and helping survivors deal with their grief. Police and soldiers prepare to kill and die to protect the public against violent assault. Secret police engage in foreign and domestic spying, but also plan assassinations and covert military assaults on foreign leaders and governments. This, of course, is done in the name of national security – policy which is designed by leaders in our federal government. Wars are threatened or waged to protect national security. Ingenious weapons of mass destruction are designed in government labs, then manufactured by private companies known as defense contractors. The large national security apparatus thrives because our leaders feel an obligation to protect our nation from attack and to preserve our way of life (including the interests of private enterprise).

Death and the Death System 85

The various institutions of the death system are societal analogues to our bodily and psychological death systems. Their function is to protect a way of life by providing for basic nourishment and survival needs, warning us against threats, sparing us from pain or worry, consoling us in our time of grieving, and preparing to violently attack external and domestic enemies. No doubt, any human society will have some sort of institutions to achieve these goals. As necessary as these institutions may be, it is also necessary to insure that they not excessively prepare for death and killing. Just as too much denial is self-destructive (and other-destructive), so too the institutions of the death system can become so powerful that they actually undermine the society they are supposed to protect. Consider some examples.

Over-fishing leads to the loss of the fish supply. Over-grazing destroys the pastureland and food supply for the grazing animals. Excessive cutting down of forests leads to loss of forest and species as well other ecological disasters.

Loss of species has an unpredictable snowball effect since one species depends on others in many ways. Industrial success leads to poisoned air, water, and soil – and to rapid global warming and destruction of the ozone layer. Without the ozone protection against ultra-violet radiation, skin cancer increases, and we could confront a world in which we suffer third degree burns and blindness. Over-doing a good thing can lead to very bad things.

With this in mind, let us examine our national security system. Its function is to serve as our nation's self-defense. To do this, it is assumed we need a strong military, a powerful secret police (for example, the CIA and FBI), government secrecy (so enemies don't know what we are up to), and a government that sometimes deceives its own citizens (because public candor could give vital information to our enemies). But what if the enemy threat our government is preparing to defend us from is exaggerated or imaginary? After all, human judgment is fallible, so perhaps our national security preparations are addressed to a level of threat that really does not exist. In response to this thought, some may defend national security preparations as follows. Okay, suppose the threat is imaginary, or perhaps the threat has been exaggerated. In that case, we still remain strong in case real threats emerge, and nothing is lost. On the other hand, if the enemy threat is real, then again we are prepared to defend ourselves and our obvious strength will likely deter any enemy attack. Either way, we win.

This kind of thinking is flawed. By allowing our government to create a super powerful security force, there is much we stand to lose. The potential for loss is great, but here are a few examples. First, other nations may perceive our "defense" preparations as excessive for true self-defense. They may interpret them as aggressive in nature if only as a means to bully other nations into serving our own self-interests. If so, they may imitate our efforts by building up their own national security forces. We may perceive their preparations as aggressive in design, leading to an arms race and a hair trigger situation where in times of conflict each nation may think they must

Death and the Death System   87

strike first before they are attacked. Such a situation is very dangerous (think of the Cold War nuclear stand off between the Soviet Union and the United States) and leads to a global instability that threatens the security of everyone involved.

A closely related hazard to maintaining a super-strong national security force is that money spent on national security will not be available for the other needs of the nation's citizenry. The Soviet Union's collapse was directly related to their excessive spending on their military. How far have we undermined our own general welfare by our government's spending on defense? Could we have used much of that money to fund education, maintain roads and transit systems, underwrite social security, day care centers, workplace safety inspection, cleaning up our polluted environment, etc? Defense contractors and their employees benefit greatly from high levels of military spending, but how much do most of us benefit from such spending?

There are other dangers to consider. A super-strong security force requires super-secrecy. Behind this veil of secrecy, there grows a powerful secret police force. Operating in great secrecy, it is hard to hold officials accountable for their mistaken judgments or corrupt actions. Citizens may be used as guinea pigs to test the effects of new weapons (for example, radioactive fallout from nuclear bombs). Huge volumes of radioactive waste may accumulate from weapons production, waste that no one knows how to keep from contaminating the world we live in. Presidents may order military or spy activities that are stupid, illegal or immoral, but no one (not even Congress) may know about them until long after the fact. If discovered, will Congress or the public have the will to hold the President (or his underlings) accountable if the action was done in the name of national defense? This actually happened with President Reagan's Iran-Contra fiasco, and Congress did not have the will to hold him accountable. If our government becomes super-strong, what will prevent their foolish or corrupt actions from violating our Constitutional rights as citizens? Will they spy on us illegally, invade our privacy, seize citizens' property without reasonable cause, arrest or detain us on trumped up charges, use their power to intimidate political dissent, etc.? This sort of thing actually happened under the Nixon presidency. Political enemy lists were established, citizens' homes and offices were burglarized and spied on, political activist organizations and leaders (including Dr. Martin Luther King) were infiltrated, etc. When the government is anxious to protect itself from perceived internal threats, the line between dissidence and subversion becomes blurred. Instead of being innocent until proved guilty in a court of law, citizens' suspicious behavior (including associating with people the government is suspicious of) indicates guilty-until-proved-innocent. As the philosopher Nietzsche wrote: "He who battles with monsters should be careful that he not become a monster."

Will our government resort to torture to pursue its war on terrorism? As President Bush pursues his War on Terrorism, there are well-documented cases of prisoner abuse in Iraq and a growing list of allegations of U.S. torture of prisoners in Iraq,

Death and the Death System 89

Afghanistan, and at the Guantanamo base in Cuba. Consider this report from Human Rights Watch:

> The torture of prisoners in US custody in Iraq was authorised and routine even after the Abu Ghraib scandal came to light, a US-based rights group says. Soldiers' accounts show that detainees routinely faced severe beatings, sleep deprivation and other abuses for much of 2003-2005, Human Rights Watch says. Soldiers who tried to complain about the abuse were rebuffed or ignored[5].

The torture allegations range from beatings to electric shock torture, and some US military personnel may face criminal homicide charges for cases where prisoners have died while under interrogation. Since 2002 there was concern in the White House that the President and other national security officials could be prosecuted for war crimes.

> The White House's top lawyer warned more than two years ago that U.S. officials could be prosecuted for "war crimes" as a result of new and unorthodox measures used by the Bush administration in the war on terrorism, according to an internal White House memo and interviews with participants in the debate over the issue. The concern about possible future prosecution for war crimes - and that it might even apply to Bush administration officials themselves - is contained in a crucial portion of an internal January 25, 2002 memo by White House counsel Alberto Gonzales

obtained by NEWSWEEK. It urges President George Bush to declare the war in Afghanistan, including the detention of Taliban and Al Qaeda fighters, exempt from the provisions of the Geneva Convention[6].

All this seems even more ominous given legal advice provided to the White House in 2003 that they were not bound by international laws which banned the torture or abuse of prisoners captured in wartime.

Bush administration lawyers contended last year that the president wasn't bound by laws prohibiting torture and that government agents who might torture prisoners at his direction couldn't be prosecuted by the Justice Department. The advice was part of a classified report on interrogation methods prepared for Defense Secretary Donald Rumsfeld after commanders at Guantanamo Bay, Cuba complained in late 2002 that with conventional methods they weren't getting enough information from prisoners. The report outlined U.S. laws and international treaties forbidding torture, and why those restrictions might be overcome by national-security considerations or legal technicalities. In a March 6, 2003, draft of the report reviewed by The Wall Street Journal, passages were deleted as was an attachment listing specific interrogation techniques and whether Mr. Rumsfeld himself or other officials must grant permission before they could be used. The complete draft document was classified

Death and the Death System 91

"secret" by Mr. Rumsfeld and scheduled for declassification in 2013. The draft report, which exceeds 100 pages, deals with a range of legal issues related to interrogations, offering definitions of the degree of pain or psychological manipulation that could be considered lawful. But at its core is an exceptional argument that because nothing is more important than "obtaining intelligence vital to the protection of untold thousands of American citizens," normal strictures on torture might not apply.[7]

Consider the new powers given to our federal government in the name of fighting terrorism. Shortly after the events of 9-11, the Congress passed legislation, known as the Patriot Act, submitted by President Bush. The law expands the power of our Secretary of State to designate groups as "terrorist" without any court or congressional review.[8] It creates a federal crime of "domestic terrorism" that broadly extends to "acts dangerous to human life that are a violation of the criminal laws" if they "appear to be intended …to influence the policy of a government by intimidation or coercion" and if they "occur primarily within the territorial jurisdiction of the United States." This broad language could easily be construed by police and prosecutors to cover vigorous, though non-violent, protests or civil disobedience. What about citizen protests against the government war policy or other government practices to pursue the war on terrorism? Think of environmental, anti-globalization, or even anti-abortion activists. Any of these could become acts of "domestic terrorism."

The Patriot Act authorized federal agents to

conduct "sneak and peak searches" or covert searches of a home or office without notifying the person of the execution of a search warrant until after the search has been completed.

The agents may also covertly seize personal items using the same justification (as in the above case) that prior notification of executing a search warrant would have an "adverse effect" if the court finds there was a "reasonable necessity" for the seizure. The FBI can covertly obtain sensitive personal information by simply certifying that doing so was for the purpose of protecting "against international terrorism or clandestine intelligence activities." It is not necessary that the FBI think that the person investigated is suspected of any wrong or illegal activities. Authorities can examine medical, financial, educational, or library records without showing any evidence of a crime. Internet providers, universities, and network administrators can be forced to turn over customer information if the FBI asserts the records are relevant to a terrorist investigation, and the company is forbidden to disclose this covert transfer to the customer. Credit reporting firms like Equifax must disclose any information the FBI requests in connection with a terrorist investigation, and without the need of a court order.

Will such power be abused? In the two months following 9-11, the Department of Justice detained over 1100 immigrants, and none of them were charged with committing acts of terrorism. A few were held as "material witnesses," and in one case a federal judge ordered a detainee set free, ruling that the case was too flimsy to merit such use of power. Secret military courts were established to try people accused of being terrorists. An office of Total Information Awareness was created to collate and monitor government and commercial databases here and abroad, which could include data on student grades, mental health and travel records. The head of this new agency said he hoped this electronic surveillance will be the most extensive in history.

Now, you might feel that these far-reaching measures are not a problem for anyone unless they have something to hide, unless they are guilty. The problem with this smug reaction is that a person need not be guilty of anything to have the government invade his or her privacy, or to be detained without charge or trial. A person need only behave suspiciously in some way. A secret police official need only believe that scouring your personal records *might* prove helpful to fighting terrorism. Maybe you know "something," say someone that *might* in some way be involved with efforts to undermine national security policy. In any event, who is not guilty of something? In searching for terrorist leads, the government may discover some information that would be very embarrassing to you. Will such information be used against you? Will the secret police begin to focus on you because of a lead from an informant, maybe a neighbor who doesn't like you or an ex-lover who is out for revenge—claiming that you have been behaving suspiciously? The secret police assigned to fight the war on terrorism at home will be under pressure to produce results. They will need to find suspicious behavior and those who might aid terrorists.

The issue of terrorism has been with us for the past thirty years. It grabbed headlines in the 1970s as airliners were skyjacked for various political motives. More recently, terrorism exploded into our consciousness through the suicide attacks on the World Trade Center Towers, the Pentagon, and the airliner that crashed in rural Pennsylvania. Suddenly, thousands of people were killed, families crippled, our economy sabotaged, and Americans' sense of security torn into tatters. Who were these barbarians filled with hate who would slaughter so many innocent civilians? As a result, President Bush declared war, even a crusade, against terrorism worldwide. He said this war would be long and difficult, and pleaded for our patience. American Forces were mobilized for protecting airports at home and to battle Osama Bin Laden and the Taliban in Afghanistan. According to President Bush, Muslim extremists under the influence of Bin Laden had committed these acts of war out of hatred for our freedom and our way of life. He and England's Tony Blair declared that we would seek out these terrorists, and those who harbored them, in order to drain their swamp and win victory over such savages. Not since the Civil War or Pearl Harbor had war come home to Americans in such stark fashion.

This war on terrorism raised many ethical questions even though everyone grants that the attacks on New York City and Washington, D.C. were extremely wrong, calling out for any surviving culprits to be held criminally accountable for their part in the mass slaughter. Some vital issues are: who was responsible for planning and carrying out

Death and the Death System 95

these attacks, and how should they be brought to justice? If and when those responsible are identified and located, how should they be punished? Another issue is: how can we best understand the motives for such hateful attacks? After all, if we do not understand what led these attacks to occur, we will be less able to prevent such attacks in the future. Perhaps, we can get nowhere before we first examine a conceptual issue. What is terrorism?

Almost all discussion of terrorism in the mass media takes for granted that terrorists attack governments or societal institutions for political reasons, but of course (as the James Bond and Die Hard movies make clear) terrorism may also be motivated by sheer greed. Someone could hijack a plane or threaten to blow up a school in order to get money and have no political cause whatsoever. Terrorists like the Unabomber or Timothy Mcveigh are the normal models we have for terrorists. They are angry at society, government agencies, or other powerful institutions, and they feel they must lash out at them in order to achieve retribution or undermine what they perceive to be very corrupt individuals or institutions. But we seldom think that governments themselves can resort to terrorism unless we think of nations that "harbor" terrorists, "terrorist States" as they are called. We surely are not accustomed to think that our own government officials could act as terrorists. But why not? Why automatically exclude government officials from fomenting or authorizing terrorism? The key objectionable moral ingredient here seems to be the use of terror to accomplish our ends. Why cannot government agents resort to this, and if they do, couldn't their actions be considered monstrous violations of the principle that the end does not necessarily justify the means? Is there any good reason why only private citizens or rebels can be thought of as committing terrorist acts? It seems arbitrary to preclude our political leaders, their allies, or "friendly agents" from the possibility of being terrorists.

What about the French government's authorizing their agents to blow up the Rainbow Warrior operated by the radical, environmental group Greenpeace? The blowing up of that ship by French secret agents resulted in the death of a Greenpeace worker. Wasn't that an act of government terrorism? In Latin America many governments have been accused by human rights organizations of sponsoring paramilitary death and torture squads. Isn't this a form of government-sponsored terrorism? In 1945 our President ordered two atomic bombs dropped on cities in Japan, first on Hiroshima and three days later on Nagasaki. The stated purpose was to bring about a quick end to the war with Japan and to achieve their unconditional surrender, but several hundred thousand civilians were killed. Was this government terrorism? Was it justified government terrorism during wartime? Did it set a precedent, an awful one, that during wartime, anything goes in order to defeat the enemy and to save lives on your own side? Recently, the government of Israel responded to the capturing of one of their soldiers by Hamas and two more soldiers by Hezbollah by relentlessly shelling and bombing Lebanon and hitting Gaza with an Iron Fist. There were many civilian casualties and deaths, including women and children. The Israelis unleashed this retaliation and terror, followed by Hezbollah launching many rockets at civilians in Israel, thereby terrorizing Israel. No doubt, neither sides' partisans would accept the claim that their actions were terrorist acts, yet from an outsider's perspective, it is clear that both are terrorizing the other for the sake of politics, revenge, and security. Finally, what about the 45-year-old Cold War between the Soviet Union and our country? Wasn't it accepted national policy during those years for both nations to feel more secure by threatening mass, nuclear terror on the other?

There seems little doubt that an individual, group, organization, or nation can wage terror on others for a variety of purposes. It can be done for money, power, self-defense, defense of allies, retribution, vengeance, paranoia, or some other reason. I propose the following definition of terrorism: acts of terror committed to achieve one's objectives. The virtue of this definition is that it is not partisan in favor of any ideology or bias. Its drawback is that it probably does not fit what most governments and people think of as terrorism. As far as I can tell, its virtue outweighs its vice, for on moral grounds, we expect our judgments to rise above bias and favoritism. After all, there is an explanation why my definition fails to fit mainstream understandings of terrorism. Active concern about "terrorism" occurs when people have had to confront such horror in real life situations, and people naturally become very emotional under such circumstances. Highly charged emotions can easily cloud clear thinking, leading to focusing piecemeal, relying on unexamined biases and neglecting broader perspective. Under such circumstances, one person's terrorist may be another person's commando or freedom fighter.

Finally, there is the general problem of how a democracy can remain faithful to its core values if the government is allowed to operate in super-secrecy. To cast a meaningful vote for a candidate, we must be accurately informed about the candidate's history and future plans. For Congress to reflect the voting public's will and carry out their Constitutional mandate, they must be accurately informed about the President's past actions and future plans. If the President acts in secret and we don't know what the President is up to, neither the public nor Congress can make informed decisions. The more the President's policy decisions and authorized actions are cloaked in secrecy, the more the democratic process is undermined and informed consent is impossible. This actually occurred under President Reagan and President Johnson's terms in office. Johnson lied to Congress and to the public about a North Vietnamese attack on two of our naval destroyers. He used this lie to gain support for expanding our war against North Vietnam and to get a Congressional resolution (The Gulf of Tonkin Resolution) which gave him the authority to do so.

Congress passed legislation expressly forbidding President Reagan from militarily attacking Nicaragua, so President Reagan did so anyway (in secret) using a secret force funded by wealthy private donors.

In the end, a healthy democracy must operate in the light of day if government officials are to be accountable to the public, their representatives, and to the rule of law. Otherwise, a powerful government operating in the shadows is a severe threat to the liberties and security of its own citizens.

1. Elisabeth Kubler-Ross, *Death Is of Vital Importance*, Station Hill Press (1995), p. 72
2. A contemporary American philosopher whose views on death (presented here) are contained in his book, *What Does It All Mean?*, Oxford University Press, 1987.
3. Thomas Nagel, *What Does It All Mean?*, Oxford University Press, 1987
4. Dr. Elisabeth Kubler-Ross, *On Death and Dying*, Simon & Schuster (1997)
5. "Iraq Prisoner Abuse Was Routine," BBC, July 23, 2006 http://news.bbc.co.uk/2/hi/americas/5206908.stm
6. "Memos Reveal War Crimes Warnings," *Newsweek*, May 17, 2004 <http://www.truthout.org/docs_04/051904A.shtml>
7. "Pentagon Report Set Framework For Use of Torture," *The Wall Street Journal*, June 7, 2004 <http://www.truthout.org/docs_04/060804A.shtml>
8. See Truth Out by J. Van Bergen, <http://www.truthout.com/docs 02/05.21B.jvb.usapa.911.htm>

Why We Should Not Torture

Torture or abusive treatment of others (including other animals) needs strong justification from a moral point of view. Normally, cruelty to those who are essentially helpless and at our mercy... is a paradigm case of what is morally evil. Torture and brutal treatment of others violates the most universal of moral rules, whether in secular or religious terms. I refer to the Golden Rule, Kant's categorical imperative, and Jesus' admonition that we are to love our neighbor as ourselves.

I shall argue that in the real world of fallible people, fallible information systems, partisan jingoism, and passions which distort human judgment—the use of torture is very likely not to promote any Greater Moral Good, hence simply to be a cruel practice without moral support and one which probably makes us less safe. We are better off without it.

Defenders of torture in all eras have appealed to the "Greater Good" to justify such cruelty. The Greater Good is the noble end which validates the use of cruel means which are normally morally unacceptable. In the past, the Greater Good was ridding society of people possessed by demons, those who practiced witchcraft, those who blasphemed God, or those who threatened the rulers of society. Today brutalizing prisoners is defended as the means to save the lives of "our own" soldiers, to save other innocent lives, or to protect society from some ghastly enemy attack. When at war, as President Bush declared we are with al Qaeda and global evildoers, extreme measures are required to fight the enemy and protect society from the enemy's violence.

From a moral point of view, the use of torture, especially as sanctioned and practiced by the State, has the opposite status of those accused of criminal crimes in the American legal tradition. A person accused of a crime is presumed innocent until proven guilty, but the use of torture is presumed wrong unless proven to be necessary for the Greater Good. We can leave aside the issue of whether the proof is to be "beyond a reasonable doubt" or "by a preponderance of the evidence." Let us simply stipulate that the standard here is "a preponderance of evidence."

Let me begin with an idealized case, one which I doubt humans are ever likely to face. Suppose there is a prisoner who the interrogator knows has information about a planned attack on a city in the USA (or elsewhere), an attack that, if carried out, will kill 200,000 civilians (men, women, and children). Furthermore, suppose it is known that if the prisoner is tortured in the most suitable way and long enough, he or she will give up this information in time to stop that terrible attack from taking place. Finally, suppose it is known that the only way to get this information from the prisoner is by using torture. Does the Greater Good here allow the torture as a morally justified action? Yes, I think so, but notice what broad implications this answer seems to have. What if Japanese interrogators in early 1945 had decided to torture an American POW to get information about the planned atomic bombings of Hiroshima and Nagasaki in August 1945?

Notice here how much knowledge we are assuming the interrogator and prisoner have. What if the prisoner has no such information? What if there is another way to get this information, either from the prisoner or otherwise? What if the torture fails to elicit the information, especially in time to stop the attack, perhaps because the prisoner dies before the information can be tortured successfully out of him or her? What if the information coerced out of the prisoner is no longer any good because those planning the attack have changed the attack plan because they believe their captured comrade will give up the information to interrogators? If any of these cases occur, the Greater Good will not be served by torturing this prisoner, and the torture will be morally wrong.

There are various reasons one might give to justify the State torture of prisoners, including revenge and to send the enemy a message about how tough "we" will be on anyone who attacks "us." Still, I think the rationale that gives many people an inclination to support State-sponsored torture is some version of the idealized case I just presented. If extreme cruelty is ever to be morally warranted, people imagine it must be to protect innocent life, to protect your "team members," or to prevent far greater suffering and death.

Knowledge seems to be the crux here. Who knows what, and how do they know it? The issue is not whether we are infallible and god-like in our ability to know things; we are not. All of us, including the interrogator and his information-support system, are fallible in judgment. The more intelligent we are, the more accurate our information-base is, the more time we have to carefully evaluate information given us, etc.—the more likely we are to arrive at a true belief or judgment.

So, let us bring this case down to Earth. A prisoner (POW or enemy combatant) is brought before interrogators, and superiors in the chain of command order the interrogators to get whatever "actionable intelligence" they can from the prisoner. Let us stipulate here that this "actionable intelligence" would be accurate and timely information about a suspected enemy large-scale attack on a US city. Is this a prisoner who actually has such information to give, or not? How are the interrogators to know? If the prisoner does not have this information, torturing him or her will not serve the Greater Good, hence be morally wrong.

For those who like detailed examinations of knowledge-issues, it would be required that the interrogator know that the sources who identify this prisoner as having such information are reliable and accurate in this case. Presumably some such information must be available, or otherwise, prisoners will, in general, be tortured simply on the grounds that they *might* have information about some such ghastly attack—even if no such attack is actually planned or any specific reason to think one is planned.

Here are some of the real life complications about being confident that the prisoner actually has such information to give. First, whoever pointed to this prisoner as a "high value information asset" might have a grudge against him or her, hence using this as an opportunity to take revenge. Likewise, the prisoner might have been identified as a likely asset because another prisoner being tortured made the claim in order to stop their own torture, on the theory that any information given might be enough to stop their own brutalization. Interrogators who suspect large-scale conspiracies are normally eager to get the identities of as many enemy conspirators as possible since they desire to disable or destroy the terror network.

Another real life problem for knowing that a tortured prisoner has "actionable intelligence" is that, once captured, his comrades may very well change the attack plan on the rational assumption that captured comrades will give up that information, hence compromising the attack plan. This means that, once captured by the enemy, whatever attack plan information a prisoner has becomes null and void—as a matter of standard operating procedure. Indeed, if the captured comrade knows anything of military value, his free comrades may want to change as much as possible, e.g. location of training camps and weapons' caches, to protect their ongoing operations. Furthermore, the captured prisoner may be too low in the organizational structure to know much, if anything, of military value to interrogators. Most national security organizations, as well as guerilla-rebel-insurgency forces, tend to operate on a "need to know basis," where only those close to the top of the pyramid know very much about plans and operations.

Furthermore, it is well known that people who are tortured will say anything they think their interrogators want to hear in order to stop the torture. How is an interrogator to know the difference between extracted information about plans for a real, large scale attack versus one simply made up by the tortured prisoner? Interrogators already suspect such attacks are planned, hence such information confirms their suspicions. You might think this can be done by seeing whether the attack occurs or does not, but this is not so. If the attack does not occur, it may either be because no such attack was really planned, because the efforts to stop it (based on the coerced information from the prisoner) succeeded, or because the attack planners changed their target or time of attack because they presumed the old plan would be compromised by interrogator torture.

If you follow the logic of the preceding paragraph, you will understand that prisoner being tortured cannot win. If they have no actionable information, they will nevertheless be tortured to see if they do have it. If they give up false information, that information will be considered a confession that they did have information which made it worthwhile to torture them. A Vietnamese woman active in the Viet Cong resistance against the oppressive government of South Vietnam said her torturers told prisoners that "if guilty, they would be tortured until they confessed, and if innocent, they would be tortured until they were guilty."

At the time of considering whether to torture a prisoner for actionable information, the question remains: is this a case where the interrogators have a justified true belief that the prisoner has actionable intelligence about the enemy, or do they simply have a mistaken hunch based on unreliable information? Does the interrogator know that the prisoner has vital information to save lots of lives, or does the interrogator simply have a mistaken belief based on unreliable sources? In the real world with all our real world ambiguities, passions, and complications—it seems unlikely that interrogators can ever be reasonably confident that a prisoner under their control has the kind of information which would justify torture as a means to the Greater Good of saving, say, 200,000 civilian lives.

Another issue is whether the torture of innocent prisoners, prisoners who have no life-saving information to give, can be morally justified where the Greater Good is a nebulous appeal to National Security. If rationally and morally warranted, this rationale will have to show that the practice of torture, even if used on innocent prisoners, will actually tend to protect the nation, and the goal of protecting the nation in question is always more important than any other matter of concern.

How will the practice of torturing innocent prisoners help protect a nation? Is the idea to show the enemy how tough "we" are, to intimidate potential enemies from "messing with us?" It is not clear how this will work realistically. For one matter, if this practice is widely known, there will also be the effect of making people outraged at such methods. Such anger and desire for retribution will create additional hostility and problems for "us." New enemies and terrorists will be created. It will also make it more unlikely that "we" will get cooperation in getting information on our enemy if others (not especially wed to our side) around the world have contempt for "our" practice of "promiscuous" torture. They may well prefer to keep helpful information to themselves rather than to assist a group they do not respect. On balance, there is a reasonable chance that the use of "promiscuous" torture of prisoners will actually harm the security of the nation using it.

Is it true that the goal of protecting one's own nation is always more important than any other concern? This view seems presupposed by any partisan who is willing to concede that the use of torture for national security will inevitably result in the abuse of innocent prisoners, yet still advocates it on the grounds that there are still a few cases where torture yields vital information. Why do the few cases outweigh the many cases of prisoner abuse unless one assumes that the lives and welfare of one's own soldiers and citizens are more valuable than the lives and welfare of others?

Whatever the case may be, this view seems morally untenable. From a moral point of view, the lives and well being of all people count equally, or at least, can be devalued only by committing moral offences. The lives of one nation's citizens are, morally speaking, no more or less valuable than those of any other nation. From a moral point of

Why We Should Not Torture 109

view, we are all entitled to a presumption of innocence until or unless there is probable cause to think we are guilty of some offence.

Overall, the idea that one nation's security is more important than any other concern is untenable. To begin with, other nations' security or welfare may be severely threatened by the dogged protection of one nation's national security. The national security and well being of Hitler's Germany threatened the security and welfare of many other nations. The same point holds for empires and civil insurrections. So what if the security of the Roman Empire or the British Empire was threatened by many societies desiring to be free of those empires? Did the security interests of Britain really have more moral weight than the desire of Indians or the American colonists to break free from British rule?

Again, it can be reasonably argued that the use of "promiscuous torture" actually undermines the national security of any nation which sanctions it. Other leaders and peoples may react with disgust and disapproval, making it more difficult to get them to cooperate with the "torture nation" in a host of ways, thus making the "torture nation" more vulnerable in a host of ways.

Finally, it seems reasonable that "we" are more likely to get useful information from prisoners (and the communities they come from) if they are treated more humanely. Approaches which avoid torture or brutality can be used to establish a rapport with the prisoner, a prisoner whose overriding desire it to be freed from captivity in order to return to a normal life with loved ones. This, combined with the well known psychological effect of prisoners coming to identify with their captors, seems far more likely to succeed than the use of torture. It is also better P-R with the world's citizenry, hence a better way to promote national security.

What's Wrong with Capital Punishment?

Here are some facts about the death penalty in our country and worldwide. 88 nations have abolished the death penalty for all crimes, while 69 retain it for some crimes. Since 1990 over 40 nations have abolished the death penalty completely. In the United States, 38 of the 50 states provide the death penalty for some crimes, and the death penalty is also allowed by military and federal law. In 2006, 53 prisoners were executed in the U.S, and 1057 prisoners had been executed in the U.S. since 1977. In 2005, 94 per cent of all known executions took place in China, Iran, Saudi Arabia and the USA. Only eight nations since 1990 are known to have executed prisoners who were under 18 at the time they were alleged to have committed a capital offense. The nations who have executed juvenile offenders are the United States, Iran, Nigeria, Pakistan, Saudi Arabia, the Congo, China, and Yemen[1]. The U.S. Supreme Court in March 2005 ruled the use of the death penalty against young people under age 18 is unlawful due to the constitutional ban against cruel and usual punishment.

The arguments for capital punishment are: retribution and deterrence. If you murder someone, *justice* (on behalf of the dead and surviving victims, and for society) requires that you too be put to death. Executing murderers sets an example for the rest of us, a deadly *lesson which will deter* others from committing murder. Some people may be willing to divorce the two rationales and settle for the deterrence rationale, but I cannot. Whatever goal or consequence-oriented rationale may be offered for capital punishment, I have little interest in the rationale if it is not restrained by principles of justice. Such approaches are dangerous and unethical.

What is murder? It is unjustified killing (among other things). Aside from torture, or torturing a person to death, no crime is more evil from a moral perspective. Innocent life deserves to be protected, and murder violates this moral dictum. But this is precisely why we should oppose capital punishment. If the death penalty is administered to people convicted of murder, innocent lives are bound to be taken.

> *Since 1973, 118 prisoners have been released from death row in the USA after evidence emerged of their innocence of the crimes for which they were sentenced to death.* Some had come close to execution after spending many years under sentence of death. Recurring features in their cases include prosecutorial or police misconduct; the use of unreliable witness testimony, physical evidence, or confessions; and inadequate defence representation. Other US prisoners have gone to their deaths despite serious doubts over their guilt. The Governor of the US state of Illinois, George Ryan,

What's Wrong with Capital Punishment

declared a moratorium on executions in January 2000. His decision followed the exoneration of the 13th death row prisoner found to have been wrongfully convicted in the state since the USA reinstated the death penalty in 1977. During the same period, 12 other Illinois prisoners had been executed[2].

Police, prosecuting attorneys, judges, witnesses[3], jurors, and public opinion are fallible and sometimes corrupt. We can sincerely, negligently, or maliciously convict people of crimes they did not commit. Such grave miscarriages of justice are documented and, in any event, are likely given the fact that human beings have imperfect judgment. Furthermore, if executions of convicted murderers are carried out more swiftly and surely (by reducing or eliminating legal appeals to murder convictions), justice will be miscarried more frequently and surely.

Some people seem to fear that we will let murderers go unpunished if we abandon capital punishment in order to make sure we spare those convicts who are truly innocent. This is a false dilemma. We are not confronted with such a terrible choice. The other alternative is to allow judges and juries the option of sentencing convicted murderers to life imprisonment without parole. This option allows us to mete out harsh punishment to those judged to deserve it without risking the execution of innocent people. This allows the State—our representative—to deliver retribution and a deterrent example without deliberately getting blood on its hands. It makes it clear to everyone in society that the state will not

[margin note: Although it is morbid to think about, could capital punishment be further justified on the grounds that it would help with the Human over-population problem on Earth?]

[margin: DCT]

sanction the extremely vengeful "eye for an eye" philosophy. In the meanwhile, as convicts serve life without parole, evidence may be uncovered which exonerates innocent convicts. In those cases, their good reputation and their liberty can be returned to them.

This seems to me a very good reason for opposing the death penalty, but some argue that there is another side to the risk of executing the innocent. They argue that there is also a risk to the innocent if we sentence convicted murderers, people who are willing to use deadly violence for no just cause, including deranged serial murderers. Since they cannot be deterred from repeat murders in prison by capital punishment, what is to prevent them from murdering other prisoners or prison employees? Such incidents have occurred. Doesn't this risk cancel out the supposed advantage of not risking the execution of innocent people? If we use capital punishment, we may execute some innocent people, but we will also prevent the true murderers from ever again committing this terrible crime.

In reply to this, I would first point out that using capital punishment does not prevent repeat murders in prison.

Unless convicted murderers are immediately executed (hence deprived of all constitutional rights of appealing their conviction or sentence), months and years will pass by before their execution, allowing time for them to murder prisoners or prison officials. Second, and more importantly, this issue is not about absolute prevention or deterrence, but justice. If we forget justice, deterrence or prevention of crime becomes a fascist strategy aimed at absolute efficiency and security. In rejecting capital punishment because it permits the state to murder innocent convicts, we are refusing to endorse the execution of the innocent. We are condemning the institution and practice as terribly unjust. To endorse capital punishment, on the other hand, is to find acceptable that officials acting on our behalf will sometimes execute an innocent person.

Compare this morally with the endorsement of life without parole as the most severe penalty allowed by law. Here we endorse a system in which none of our public officials is allowed to willfully execute anyone, hence innocent convicts are spared being murdered by our representatives. Now in such an alternative system, we expect that all reasonable and humane precautions will be taken by the prison system to minimize the chance that prison officials, employees or prisoners will be brutalized by anyone in the system. Still, this risk cannot be eliminated absolutely. For example, prisoners who are especially violent and dangerous should be placed in solitary confinement, but even so, some may still commit acts of brutality or murder. Even though such acts are rare, they may still occur, which means that the life-without-parole system will make possible the murder of innocent people within the prison system. To this extent, there is a parallel evil associated with both capital punishment and life without parole. Both practices allow that, given their goals, the murder of innocent people is a necessary risk. But here the parallel ends. In the case of capital punishment, the practice means that representatives of the public, i.e. prison officials and employees, are approved to carry out the execution of convicted murderers, whether or not they are innocent. The public's representatives do the killing, which means the murdering in cases where the convicts are innocent. In the case of life without parole, it is not our prison employees or officials who do the killing, but prisoners. Here the murder of innocent people is in no way endorsed as an instrument of public will or policy.

In the final analysis, I think the overall rightness or wrongness of capital punishment hinges on justice: is this technique a just way to carry out justice? Even if the convict is guilty of murder, does justice require that he or she be executed by the State?

Let us begin by considering the "eye for an eye" rationale. First, to act on it thoroughly and consistently, it seems the State must treat murderers precisely as they treated their victims. Notice, first of all, that in cases where the murderer acted out of extreme passion in the heat of the moment, it will not be possible for the State to mimic their crime—for the State will have to execute them with premeditation and not in the heat of the moment. In other words, killing in cold blood is morally distinct from killing in hot blood. Hence, the punishment is not "precisely" a payback. Next, if the murder was done with premeditation, was it accomplished by strangulation, the knife, a gun, poison, bare fists, or torture? Whichever the technique, should the State employ it likewise against the murderer if an "eye for an eye" is to be extracted? Surely, this kind of retribution would set an example of great cruelty and brutality, a terrible "moral" message.

In any event, I think many of those who support capital punishment would think it necessary to go to this extreme.

Even in the *Old Testament* (*Exodus 21*), a tit for tat response to all wrongdoing is not recommended. An eye for an eye is to be applied fairly literally in the case of serious wrongdoings involving murder and other harm done intentionally to a person's body, but for other sorts of wrongdoing, the punishment should not be so literally tit for tat. For example, for recklessly striking a pregnant woman, causing her to give birth prematurely, the offender should be fined in an amount determined by the woman's husband. Also, if one man physically assaults another, causing injury and temporary disability, the offender deserves to be fined.

What is good about the "eye for an eye" principle is that it attempts to keep the response to wrong-doing proportional to the wrong-done. After all, people can feel that when an injury is done to them, they are entitled to extract "many eyes for one eye." Feelings of righteous indignation can lead to excessive retaliation against wrong-doers. In this respect, the "eye for an eye" principle is morally progressive. We are still called on to interpret the meaning of an "eye for an eye." I suggest that its most generic meaning is that severe wrong-doing merits severe punishment, mild wrong-doing merits mild punishment, and actions in the vast middle between these extremes deserve a "middle-ground" punishment. I think most people would agree that we need not punish severe wrong-doers by harming them exactly like they harmed the victim. That is, we need not kill murderers exactly in the way they killed their victims. Likewise, fining a person $20 for murdering someone is a morally inappropriate response. Still, the real issue here is whether life in prison (without parole), execution, or some other punishment is harsh enough to satisfy the proportionality requirement of justice-done. For the moment, I simply point out that, in a generic sense, this proportionality requirement is satisfied if the punishment for a severe crime is also severe.

The deep incoherence of an extreme interpretation of the "eye for an eye" policy is as follows. Since the murderer killed without justification, so too must the state execute the murderer without justification. Remember, 'murder' is not synonymous with killing. If the alleged murder was done with justification, the killing was not murder, and it would be wrong to execute the killer. The killing must have been unjustified, and an "eye for an eye" requires that the murderer's execution be done without justification. But this policy is rationally incoherent. We should never do *anything* which is unjustified. To imply that one wrong act requires another wrong act to counterbalance it is to open a Pandora's box of intellectual maggots. For example, since the murderer killed an innocent person, perhaps the state should react by executing not the murderer, but some innocent person(s) who the murderer cares for –e.g. a spouse, parent, or child. Here lies the way to madness, but it would be consistent with the "eye for an eye" philosophy.

I think what the above indicates is that it is not obvious or clear what the meaning of an "eye for an eye," (just retribution) is. Presumably, if morally relevant, it expresses the principle that there needs to be a proportionate response to moral evil. Our response to evil deeds must be restrained. We cannot, for example, take two eyes for one eye. This would be an overreaction and morally unjustified. Nor should we respond to murder with the response we have to shoplifting. To do so would be to take the crime of murder far too lightly (or the crime of shoplifting far too gravely). There must be balance and proportion in our responses to various moral transgressions.

Since just retribution is a literal tit for tat response to wrongdoing (stealing a car from a thief who steals a car, a male who rapes a female being raped by the female he raped, etc.), I suggest that the best and most general interpretation of retribution is the following principle: the degree of harm done by the wrongdoer should be reflected in the degree of harm in his or her punishment. Severe wrongdoing merits severe punishment, and mild wrongdoing merits mild punishment. According to this understanding of justice, the severe crime of murder merits a severe punishment, but the exact nature of this punishment is left open for us to decide. Since the sentence of life in prison without parole is a severe punishment, such a penalty for murder is consistent with meting out just retribution to the convicted offender.

This brings me to the other venerable rationale for capital punishment: deterrence. Execution is imagined to deter the murderer from ever again committing murder, and to deter others from murder. Although I have no objection to punishment as a way to deter immoral behavior, I do doubt that the death penalty achieves this goal in a rational and ethical manner. While killing the murderer clearly prevents him or her from ever again killing, the certainty of this solution does not mean it is the best solution. After all, if deterrent certainty is our paramount goal, we can prevent individuals from ever again stealing, breaking their agreements, drinking under age, or speeding by executing them after their first violation. If we respect justice, punishment must be a balanced means of achieving deterrence. Effectiveness of stopping the repetition of a crime is not the moral bottom-line.

The other goal of deterrence is to prevent others from committing the offence in the future. Reduction or elimination of such violations is the goal. Does capital punishment work for this purpose? I am no scholar of the empirical studies on this subject, but the ones I am aware of do not support capital punishment's effectiveness. In Canada homicide rates have dropped 40% since capital punishment was abolished in 1975. The most recent survey of research findings on the relation between the death penalty and homicide rates, conducted for the United Nations in 1988 and updated in 2002, concluded:

> . . .it is not prudent to accept the hypothesis that capital punishment deters murder to a marginally greater extent than does the threat and application of the supposedly lesser punishment of life imprisonment[4].

What's Wrong with Capital Punishment 121

In any case, we need to know whether the death penalty is a more effective deterrent than life imprisonment without parole. Often such comparisons have not been the basis for empirical studies. Instead, studies have simply compared those areas which have capital punishment and those that do not—whether or not they allow for the parole of convicted murderers.

My deep skepticism about the deterrence of the death penalty comes from other considerations. First, I doubt that it is the death penalty which would deter. I think it would be the knowledge that murderers are almost always caught, found guilty, and surely executed. In other words, the rational gambler in many of us will allow us to risk suffering severe harm so long as we believe (1) the harm is not likely, and (2) we are strongly motivated to continue the risky behavior. Cigarette smokers are good examples of this point. Now, someone contemplating murdering someone would be reasonable if they were skeptical that (a) the police usually get "their man" in homicide investigations, (b) the murderer is always convicted and sentenced to death, (c) the conviction is never overturned to appeal, (d) the convict is never granted a pardon, or (e) the death sentence is never commuted. Furthermore, the person contemplating murder may have strong, positive reasons for committing such a drastic act—e.g. personal revenge or money. With all this in mind, I don't think we can reasonably expect people to be deterred simply by the legal possibility the death penalty *might* be applied to them.

To overcome this problem, we would (at a minimum) need to make law enforcement improvements which would lead reasonable folks to know that murderers are usually caught and executed by the state. Though death penalty advocates would no doubt applaud the idea of making law enforcement super-efficient, I have indicated why this would lead more innocent people to be more frequently executed, hence is unacceptable. Furthermore, making police this powerful would jeopardize all of our civilian rights in other ways as well – e.g. threats to our liberty and privacy due to corrupt abuses of power. Finally, this strategy would do nothing to deter the many people who murder not out of premeditation, but impulsively out of the passion of the moment.

I am also concerned about the kind of example we set if our society promotes the execution of convicted murderers. I believe the lesson we teach is morally terrible, namely "the criminal justice system in this country is founded on violence. It is a system which assumes that violence can be overcome by violence, evil by evil. Criminal justice at home and warfare abroad are the same principle of violence. This principle sadly dominates much of our criminology."[5] Death penalty-advocates hope to teach people that murderers forfeit their right to life and deserve to be executed by the appropriate officials in prescribed ways. I think this hope is naïve. Consider the facts, then consider what people will infer from these facts. A person is found guilty of murder, is sentenced to die for the wrongful killing, and the State condones this and carries out the prescribed execution. What will reasonable people infer?

Surely, some will infer that the lesson here is an "eye for an eye." If so, they have learned something which is dangerous to society. Whether they infer "one killing deserves another" or "one unjustified killing deserves another unjustified killing," they will be entitled to infer that the State's killing of the convict requires a further killing. This lesson endorses an indefinite tit-for-tat cycle of revenge. Friends and loved ones of the executed convict would be justified to conclude that the State executioner and the authorizing authorities deserve to be killed.

Of course, death penalty-advocates can insist that it is only the state acting lawfully that can legitimately carry out executions. This is futile. The more this rationale is urged, the more likely other people are to conclude that the real underlying principle is "might makes right" or that this is an arbitrary defense of the status quo. If so, respect for lawful authority will be further undermined. If many people interpret the lesson here to be, "a killing-solution is best for a killing-problem," the security and welfare of society will be further damaged. People will decide for themselves whether premeditated execution is arbitrary when carried out by a private citizen, but justified when done by the State.

What separates a justified killing from a murder? It must be a drastic remedy of last resort; there must be no reasonable alternative. Such killing must occur in order to defend life against severe assault, especially against the threat of death. Furthermore, the threat of life must be imminent, or at least very likely in the foreseeable future—not just imagined or possible in the indeterminable future. Are these constraints met in the case of state executions of convicted murderers? Of course, they are not met in those cases where the convicts are really innocent. So we must focus on executions of those who really are guilty of murder. I have argued there is a reasonable punishment alternative to the death penalty, and if I am right, capital punishment does not meet the conditions for appropriate deterrence.

Still, there are other cases to consider. First, are the lives of the executioner and those who authorize the execution in clear jeopardy? Second, are other citizens' lives in clear jeopardy from the convicted murderer? Third, is society itself in clear jeopardy from the convicted murderer? If, in any of these three cases, clear or present danger does exist, executing the convict could qualify as justified killing. Consider the first case. A convict will rarely be in a position to gravely threaten the lives of the executioner or those who authorize the execution, hence this case will almost always be moot. Consider the second case. Once in prison, convicts will normally be in a poor position to assault anyone except prison guards or fellow prisoners. Since solitary confinement is always an option for especially violent convicts, the prospects of a convict posing this kind of clear threat will be very small. If, on the other hand, the use of deadly violence against a convict is necessary to repel their assault on a prison guard, fellow prisoner, or anyone else, so be it! But we do not execute convicted murderers for this reason; capital punishment is the premeditated killing in cold blood of a convict who has been rendered defenseless.

What about the third case? Will our society likely collapse if we end capital punishment? Hardly. Relatively few people actually attempt to murder others, and assuming we impose life sentences without parole for certain murders, people will have strong incentives for not jumping on the murder bandwagon. Furthermore, victims' desires for retribution or revenge will not be neglected (though many will, no doubt, prefer the death penalty). Finally, keeping the death penalty may well pose a greater risk to society's security and well being because it teaches a lesson of tit-for-tat, open-ended revenge.

In conclusion, I see no motives beyond fear and vengeance which can serve to prop-up the practice of capital punishment. Neither justice nor deterrence is well served by this practice. If someone I loved were murdered, I might well feel enough grief and hatred to desire the murderer's execution. I am human, but such grief and hatred cannot serve as a rational justification. Being in such states of disturbing passion are the paradigms of contexts which produce imbalanced judgment. They tend to make us lose perspective and our sense of fairness. We must hold on to the ideal of impartiality and objectivity precisely for those cases where we are most tempted to abandon them. I believe justice and love should guide every society if we are to be the best we can be. The practice of capital punishment makes our society more cruel and violent, and it executes both justice and love.

1. According to Amnesty International, "Facts and Figures on The Death Penalty." (online, 2001, 2004 and 2008) <http://thereport.amnesty.org/eng/Facts-and-Figures>
2. http://web.amnesty.org/rmp/dplibrary.nsf/ff6dd728f6268d0480256aab003d14a8/46e4de9d b9087e35802568810050f05f!OpenDocument, http://web.amnesty.org/library/Index/ENGACT500122004?open&of=ENG-392. Also, "The Death Penalty Worldwide...," http://web.amnesty.org/library/Index/ENGACT500012005?open&of=ENG-392
3. DNA testing is showing an increasing number of convicts (whether concerning murder, rape, or other offenses) to be innocent. There have been 100 exonerations since 1989. One man convicted of rape largely on the basis of eyewitness testimony served nearly 20 years before being exonerated. ("Increasing DNA exonerations contradict predictions," *USA Today*, 8A, 1-18-2002)
4. These statistics about Canada and conclusion of a U.N. sponsored survey are from Amnesty International on line: http://web.amnesty.org/library/Index/ENGACT500122004?open&of=ENG-392, http://web.amnesty.org/library/index/ENGACT500082004
5. R. Quinney as quoted by R. Craig in "The Search for Justice in An Unjust World: John MacMurray and Criminal Justice," *Journal for Peace and Justice Studies* (Vol. 9, 1), 65

Searching for Democracy

We know we are the most powerful nation on the face of the Earth, the most powerful country in history. We are proud of our power and our values, especially our democracy and the commitment to freedom and human rights. For most, our self-image as citizens of the United States of American is very positive and deeply rooted. We think of ourselves as truly living in "the land of the free and the home of the brave," a nation we pledge to be under God with liberty and justice for all. We have our problems as a nation, and we can improve, but we are far better off as citizens of the U.S.A. than living in any other country. We live in America, where "God shed His grace on thee," a nation where all citizens have the opportunity to be successful, where a child born to poverty can become a millionaire, and where a child from humble origins can become President.

We also are righteous warriors and protectors of people all over the world. We keep our troops posted all over the world to fight the enemies of freedom. The evildoers should know that (as the old song says) "The Yanks are coming, and we won't stop fighting 'til it's over, over there." We have proved this commitment from the 19th century until the present by sending our military or covert operatives to Central and South America, to

Europe, to Asia, and to Africa. Our troops patrol the air and the oceans of the planet. We make mistakes, but no one should doubt our noble motives to defend and spread freedom in the world. Our democracy is not perfect, but it is the best ever to exist, and our nation is the best in the world. Those who doubt this are either ignorant or the malicious enemies of freedom.

(Amen. The congregation may be seated.)

For many, America is more than a homeland; it is a shining dream, something close to a secular religion. Indeed, there are Christian "reconstructionists" who would like to replace the *Constitution* with the *Bible* as the Supreme Law of our land. They want to make it true that the U.S.A. is ruled "on earth as it is in heaven." Others, whether they are religious or not, don't want to turn the American dream into a theocracy, but they are devoted to the dream as if guarding a magical treasure. Some may call them "idolaters," but many Americans are devoted to "America-right-or-wrong-Love-it-or-leave-it!" even as others are devoted to God, Allah, or Jesus Christ.

I grew up with this faith and devotion to America. I was born and raised in Wyoming by Republican parents. I never doubted that American was the glorious bastion of liberty, human rights, prosperity, justice and equality. It wasn't until the Kennedy assassination and the Vietnam War escalation of the mid 60s that I began to have some doubts. After my second year of college, I would never again feel kinship with Christian soldiers marching off to war.

Once you begin to notice things that don't fit, oddities parading as normalcy, suddenly it seems as though oddities are popping up all over the place. It is almost like waking from a dream, now noticing words written in plain black and white which formerly were camouflaged in lemon oil. Consider that in our Pledge of Allegiance, we pledge ourselves to the flag first and only afterward "to the Republic for which it stands." This smacks of flag fetishism, the secular equivalent of idolatry. It is also strange that our nation did so well for nearly 200 years without having any such patriotic pledge. Why was it in the 1940s and 1950s that Americans became so needy of pledging themselves to flag and republic? Indeed, why did it become urgent to include "one nation under God" in that pledge? Was there something about winning World War 2 or embarking on a Cold War with the Soviet Union that made Americans feel insecure and in need of a flag to protect them? Were our citizens worried that patriots no longer believed in God or that God no longer blessed America? Having only been born in 1948, I can only speculate about the swirling forces of psyche and politics that led to this urgency. Being barely aware at the time, I do recall being marched around in Sunday school while the lead children held aloft cross and flag, as we all sang "Onward Christian soldiers, marching off to war, with the cross of Jesus, going on before."

Second to the flag, our Pledge commits us to honor our republic "indivisible with liberty and justice for all." What is a "republic?" There are two related meanings of this term. One is about a nation ruled not by a king or queen, a nation not governed by royalty. The other is about a nation governed for the sake of the people, for the sake of the public good (from the Latin, meaning a "public thing"). Our nation certainly is a republic in the first sense. Much as some might wish it otherwise, we have no king or queen. We fought against King George for an independent nation free from the rule of monarchy, but are we a nation (in the second sense of "republic") whose government is devoted to the good of the public? True, our Constitution proclaims (in the Preamble) that our nation is committed to "We, the People," but is our government really devoted to promoting "the general welfare?" Is our government devoted to protecting "liberty and justice for all?"

To answer this, we must turn to another virtue we claim for our republic—democracy. The idea of democracy was invented and implemented (to some degree) in Athens, Greece over 2000 years ago. Democracy is rule by and for the people. Is our nation ruled by and for the people? Probably many of us think we are a democracy because we are allowed to vote and indeed have the legal right to vote. Probably many think we must be a democratic country because we have lots of personal freedom and we have a Bill of Rights to give legal protection to us against government abuses. These are worthy points, but we must remember that even in the old Soviet Union, citizens had the right to vote. The problem was that they could only vote yes or no, and they could only vote for members of the Communist Party. As for our Bill of Rights, the rights we are legally guaranteed are indeed true marks of the democratic spirit, but such legal rights are not worth much if they are not enforced, protected, and used in practice. We must guard against revering our Castle in the Sky while living in hovels beside it. Many Americans seem hostile to the American Civil Liberties Union, yet the ACLU is devoted to protecting people's Constitutional rights. Do we stand up for our Constitutional rights in this country? Does our government seek to honor and protect these rights? Such questions must be asked and answered thoughtfully if we are to understand the extent to which basic human rights are protected or neglected in our great land.

We must also be wary of being led astray here by a seductive vision of direct versus representative democracy. Ancient Athenians in the time of Pericles had a government in which the free citizens of Athens met daily to debate and vote on the pressing issues of their city-state. When they voted to have certain civic projects accomplished, the citizens were voting to carry out those projects themselves, not others they elected to represent them. This is what is called "direct democracy," and it is often portrayed as though it is the pure or perfect form of democracy. As human societies grew in population and complexity, another form of democracy was adopted by the United States, France, and certain other nations around the world. In this kind of democracy, citizens voted to have other citizens represent their interests in government. This modern form of democracy is known as "representative democracy," and it is usually portrayed as the imperfect, but practical, version of the old Athenian style of government. The seduction here is thinking that the basic distinction is between direct-perfect democracy versus representative-imperfect democracy. This way of thinking conceals more than it reveals. The ancient Athenian democracy was not perfect and was arguably not "democracy" at all. The benchmark of democracy is not whether the government is handled directly by the voting citizens; the benchmark is whether the rule is by and for the people.

Was ancient Athens ever ruled by and for the people? Here our standard must be the extent to which real societies implement ideals. We cannot expect in our real world that citizens or governments will ever be perfect in their motivation or the way they carry out their duties. That benchmark would be unreasonable. To be reasonable, we can expect that to qualify for a society ruled "by and for the people," the decisions are made by a majority of the citizens and motivated usually by what is best for the general welfare. If we find a society claiming to be democratic, but where the decisions are normally made by a minority of the voting age citizens, we can reasonably reject that society as "democratic." Is our republic ruled by the majority of its voting age citizens? Do we have a history of such majority rule? As for the motives of people in our government, here we must make a practical inference since it is problematic to read people's minds. We must judge that the people who actually make decisions about government will, at least, normally be rational agents who attempt to do what they consider to be in their best interest and those things they care about. Thus, if everyone in government happened to have been professional educators, it is reasonable to assume they would try to do what is best for them and what promotes education in their society.

Using this benchmark, we can say decisively that Athenian "democracy" was not remotely close to perfect, although it was direct in style. Women could not vote or hold office. The Athenian economy rested on slavery, especially slaves to mine silver for making their famous Attica owl coins. Only adult (free) males could vote and serve in governing Athens. This means that old Athens was not governed by a majority of its people, yet the majority certainly contributed greatly to the functioning of Athens. Resting on patriarchy and slavery, Athens was a deeply flawed democracy, even though it was a direct form of government. Furthermore, since decisions did not reflect the input of most of its voting age public, it can be reasonably claimed that old Athens was not a democracy at all. To be a genuine democracy, a nation must be governed, at a minimum, by majority rule. After that base line is met, we can talk about the degree to which a nation is democratic or not, using:

- the percentage of public participation
- customs and traditions to encourage maximum voter participation, protection of human rights, etc.

In any case, we can safely conclude, ancient Athens was either a very imperfect democracy or no democracy at all. Ancient Athens may have contained the seeds of democracy, but we cannot use it as our ideal model.

What about the representative form of government we have in our United States of America? Everyone grants that our government is not a perfect democracy, but is it democracy at all? To what extent have we been ruled by "We, the People?"

Our nation was born in the late 18th century, 1776 or 1789, depending on which events you consider most important in our birthing process. It was a painful and violent birth as we demanded our independence from England. As a young nation, we are now over two centuries old, still in our infancy as far as the life of nations goes. Though some may think it not very relevant to examine our nation from birth to present, it should be remembered that the character of a nation is not judged by the present and recent past, but by its values and behavior over its entire lifetime. The values and actions that, as a rule, dominate our history up to the present are what give us our character as a nation. Just as a person is not considered lazy simply because they infrequently are lazy, but only because they are normally lazy, so too a nation is not judged by its exceptional behavior, but by its normal behavior. So, looking into our distant past is not just exploring "ancient history," but is instead an effort to gain an overall and balanced view of our society and its government. We know that the circumstances one is born into, for better or worse, normally have a powerful effect on one's future development.

The original 13 States were dominated by patriarchy and property, including slavery. Women could not vote, and neither could African slaves,

Indians, indentured servants, or poor people. A majority of voting age citizens were not permitted to vote, much like was true in the old Athenian "democracy." The rule of a nation by a minority is not democracy, but oligarchy. This was the character of our nation for many years to come. In 1865, slavery and indentured servitude were finally abolished, and five years later, we made it illegal to exclude people from voting based on their race or previous condition of servitude. Women would have to wait 131 years until 1920 to be allowed to vote, the result of a strong women's suffrage movement. Poor people in many Southern states would have to wait until 1964 before poll taxes and "civics" tests (to preclude poor folks, especially poor blacks from voting) were made illegal. Thus, techniques to disenfranchise the poor and the black were in effect for 175 years. Putting these simple numbers into perspective, this means that for more than half of our nation's existence, women could not vote and it was impossible for many poor people of color to vote.

Consider too the original Constitution which served as our nation's Supreme Law. Pundits and scholars are fond of emphasizing the checks and balances in our Constitution, checks and balances on the power that the three branches of government have on one another. Less mentioned is the check placed on the power of the people. The Constitution originally mandated that the President be elected by special electors chosen by each of the 13 State legislatures in whatever manner they saw fit. Their majority vote determined who would be President, and if no candidate voted on by them received a majority of their votes, the Congress was to vote on which of those candidates was to be President. The public was to have no direct vote for whom they preferred as the next President.

Since our nation's birth, this system has changed slightly, but the decision for who is elected President still remains in the hands of the electors. Each State is awarded a number of electors equal to the number it has in Congress: two senators and a certain number of representatives. Each candidate for President has a number of people ready to server as his or her electors from that State in the event of the candidate's receiving most of the votes cast in that State's vote for President. The Presidential candidate who receives the largest popular vote in that State has his or her entire slate of electors chosen to cast that State's vote for President. This means that when the popular vote for President is fairly close, it can happen that the person selected for President is not the person who receives the most popular votes nationwide. This has happened several times in our history, and it happened as recently as the Presidential election of 2000 when Al Gore won the nationwide popular vote, but lost the election to George W. Bush. This "electoral college" system is just one more built in mechanism to prevent our nation from being ruled by the people.

So far, it would seem our nation is either a very flawed democracy, or it is not a democracy at all. Supposing our goal is to be "ruled by the people," how could our system be changed so that it came closer to the benchmark of majority rule? How could we make our nation more democratic, or (to speak more strictly) how could we get closer to being a genuine democracy? We can begin here with where we just left off. We could put an end to the "electoral college" system for selecting our President and Vice President. We could elect our President on the principle of a nationwide, direct election, basing this on a one person-one vote philosophy. This would require that our Constitution be amended, and this is simply not likely to happen. There are too many people that feel that this old system works well enough, and both parties at the national level are content to hang on to the Electoral College.

Failing this, we could revise our formula for selecting electors for the Presidential election. This could be done without abandoning the Electoral College. To do this, we would abandon the old "winner takes all principle" and assign electors according to the proportion of vote their candidate receives in each State. Thus, if there were two candidates running in a State with 20 total electoral votes, and candidate A received 60% of the popular vote in that State, candidate A would receive 12 electoral votes from that State, and the other candidate would receive 8 electoral votes. Under the current system, the 40% of the voters in this case have their votes treated exactly the same as if they had not voted at all. This is very undemocratic. This also encourages citizens to cast their votes only if they are fairly sure they will vote for the winning candidate. If they vote for the winner, their vote has some weight. If they vote for the loser (in the winner-takes-all system), their vote has the value of zero. The rest of the electoral system for selecting our President would remain the same. Whichever candidate received a majority of the electoral votes cast would be selected as President. In the event of a tie, or a case where no candidate wins a majority of the electors' votes cast, the Congress would choose the next President (just as it now says in Amendment 12 to our Constitution). Although this too is unlikely to happen, Congress could make it so by changing statutory federal election law. At present, there seems to be no political will by the national GOP or DEMS to move in this direction. As the old saying goes, it is hard to teach old dogs new tricks.

If we wanted to take a further step toward making each person's vote count, we could give voters even more choice when they cast their vote in elections where there were three or more candidates on the ballot. At present, in such cases, voters have to choose to vote for one of the candidates to the exclusion of all the others, but in many cases, this limitation will not accurately reflect many voters' preferences. For example, suppose there were three candidates on the ballot in the presidential election: Tweedledum, Tweedledee, and Darth Vader. Many voters might prefer Tweedledee slightly over Tweedledum, but prefer both immensely more than Darth Vader. Their honest ranking of the three candidates would be better reflected by saying Tweedledee is their first choice, Tweedledum is their second choice, while Darth Vader is a distant third choice. To allow for this sort of ranking to be reflected on ballots, voters (rather than simply voting for Tweedledee rather than the other two) would indicate #1 for Tweedledee, #2 for Tweedledum, and #3 for Darth Vader. What each voter would

Searching for Democracy

thereby be indicating is that if Tweedledee cannot receive a majority/plurality of the vote, they would much prefer Tweedeledum to be elected rather than Darth Vader. If most voters do not prefer Tweedledum as their #1 choice, this will not necessarily mean that Darth Vader is elected, because most voters may rank Tweedledum ahead of Vader. Suppose, for the sake of simplicity, that there are only ten voters who vote in this election. If so, the following could be the result for this 3-way race for President. ['X' means no number was assigned by that voter for that candidate.]

Voter	Rank for each Candidate		
	Tweedledee	Tweedledum	Vader
Frank	1	2	3
Ray	1	2	3
Barry	3	2	1
George	3	2	1
John	3	2	1
April	1	2	3
Brittany	2	3	1
Madonna	1	2	3
Hillary	1	2	3
Condolezza	X	X	1

Now, there is the possibility that one of these three candidates will receive 10 first place votes, but in this case, the electorate split evenly their #1 preferences between Tweedledee and Vader with neither candidate receiving a majority of the votes cast. On the other hand, 80% of the voters' preferences for #2 went to Tweedledum. (Notice too that Condolezza chose not to rank her votes except to say that she wanted Vader or no one. That vote would be perfectly okay within the system under consideration here. The idea is to give voters more choice, not to force it on them.) In this imaginary election, Tweedledum would be elected President because he was ranked higher by a majority of the voters than the other two. As you can see, Darth Vader was a polarizing candidate with half of the voters ranking him their most favorite candidate and half ranking him their least favorite candidate.

If you want to engage your imagination here, suppose this electoral system had been in place in the Presidential election of 2000. How might that election have turned out if voters could have ranked George Bush, Al Gore, and Ralph Nader as their first, second, or third preference?

Would the results have been the same? Might Nader have been elected President? Could he have been the #2 choice of a majority of the voters? Of course, we will never know. We can say, however, that if this progressive voting system had been in effect, it would not have made sense to accuse Nader of being the "spoiler candidate," because voters would not have had to decide simply to vote for one candidate or not vote at all. They would have been able to rank the three candidates instead of being forced to choose one candidate over the others in an absolutist way.

There are other things we could do to "tweak" our election system to make it more democratic. We could hold elections at times to make it very convenient for citizens to vote: over a weekend Saturday and Sunday, in the summer, or on a day declared a national holiday. In Germany, civil servants are given two days off to count the paper ballots (they only use paper), but the citizens know very quickly who won due to the use of exit polls. Those exit polls have been astonishingly accurate in Germany for decades. This shows that moving to more computerized voting machines, as has been the trendy response in America to the voting debacle of 2000 in Florida, is not necessarily the right way to have integrity and speedy results in elections. High tech is not always indicated as a path to progress. Indeed, it can be a step backward. Computerized voting machines with no paper trail as an independent record of voters' choices can be manipulated and lead to massive election fraud.

We should move far away from the private financing of elections. Clean and fair elections require that all major candidates receive public funding for their campaigning, and also that the playing field be level. Each candidate would have the same spending limits for the election campaign. The idea is to have elections where citizens cast their votes for candidates based on the candidates' ideas and character, not according to which candidate has paid for the most overwhelming and glitzy campaign ads. We want all candidates to have name recognition, not some more than others due to expensive P-R campaigns. If a voter wants to vote for a candidate because the candidate is rich, that is fine, but the wealthy should not be able to determine who has a chance to be seen and heard by the voters. To preserve integrity and openness of the election process, all candidates should play on a level playing field; each should have the same amount of funds to expend on their campaign. This means that whether they are privately or publicly financed, each candidate should have the same spending limit for their campaign. If this is not done, those candidates backed by more money will have an unfair advantage over the other candidates, and indeed many will not become candidates simply because they do not have the backing of enough wealth.

The wealthy may feel that such reform unfairly disadvantages them because the great majority of citizens are not wealthy, hence can use their overwhelming numbers to outvote the wealthy-minority class. These fears of the wealthy have some merit, but protections can be built into the system to protect them against being "plundered" by the majority, and in any case, this is the price of true demo-cracy. Rule by and for the people is not about special protections for the wealthy. If the wealthy cannot live with democracy, they should live elsewhere.

The prospects of gaining this sort of electoral reform are very slim. The influence of big money is too widespread and powerful in our society to expect much progress on this score. Aside from lots of lip service to the value of democracy, what really moves our culture is football, celebrity, the entertainment industry, personal liberty, and the chase for money and power. We can judge a nation's character by what it most values. If we were to erect a shrine to our secular holy trinity, it would be the shrine of Football, Liberty, and the Almighty Dollar.

One very powerful industry is the business of TV broadcast news, information and entertainment. Companies like CBS, ABC, NBC, MSNBC, CNN, and Fox News bring us the news of the day, and the great majority of our citizens depend on TV news for the information they get about the world and our domestic political scene. No political candidate running at the state or national level can hope to succeed without his or her campaign being covered by our TV media. These companies depend, for a large part of their revenue, on the money they gain from parties and candidates paying to run their campaign ads on TV. These media outlets are addicted to political campaign money. Surely, the TV networks will lobby heavily against any changes in our political campaigns which reduce the money they are used to making during political campaigns. Who will Congress listen to most closely? To those whose voices cry out for progressive democratic reform, or to those who pay TV network bills?

We should not be surprised that most Americans do not vote or follow politics in any serious way. As citizens, we are encouraged to do almost everything but be involved in our political process. Consider those institutions which are most formative for attitudes and habits. Beginning with our family and parents, the problem is already entrenched. Most parents don't vote or choose to become politically involved, and in any event, families are not run democratically. Parents decide and children are expected to obey (parents rule and children drool). Next, we encounter Church, Sunday School, and regular school K-12. Neither are these institutions run democratically. Each is in varying degrees authoritarian and hierarchical. Once in the work force, matters will not change. Owners, CEOs, and supervisors decide, and the employees are to obey. The process is almost wholly top-to-bottom and non-democratic. If a person joins the armed forces, of course, the entrenched authoritarian process will only be deeper.

If our mainstream institutions are non-democratic, exactly how are most Americans supposed to gain the desire to be players in the great game of democracy? Indeed, it is almost miraculous that so many Americans do get involved in one way or another. It is not surprising, however, that we are lucky to get a 50% turnout of registered voters for our Presidential elections. An immense number of our citizens seem deeply estranged from the electoral process. They don't trust the System. A recent Zogby Poll (of over 8000 Americans, age 18-24) found that 75% trusted the government less now that they did five years ago. Only 5% said that corporations "do right" by consumers. Only 25% feel the print and broadcast news media gives us fair and accurate information. All three branches of the federal government are deemed untrustworthy:

Congress 3%, President 24%, Judiciary 29%[1]

?: what would be some of your own personal suggestions to increase voter turnout in America?

These kinds of poll results tend to undermine the cynical view, widely held among intellectuals, that most Americans don't participate simply because they are lazy and apathetic. Such a smug conclusion is, no doubt, also comforting to those who clearly benefit from the established order and status quo, but a more reasonable interpretation is that most citizens are alienated from their government and news dissemination process. Given such attitudes in the populace, it is no surprise that they choose not to get very involved in the electoral process. It seems likely that most Americans do not feel their voice counts for much in deciding how they are governed. Neither do they feel that mainstream news media provide them with reliable information, so how can they feel optimistic that their decisions are informed by facts rather than fiction or propaganda? It is a sad joke among many progressives that after our government finishes spreading democracy to the rest of the world, maybe they will do the same here for the United States. As the comedian, Steven Colbert, has suggested, maybe our nation is less devoted to democracy than it is to demo-crazy.

1. *U.S. Public Widely Distrusts Its Leaders*, Zogby Poll, May 23, 2006, http://www.zogby.com/news/ReadNews.dbm?ID=1116

On Our Own Again: Searching for Meaning

The term 'existentialism' was a grab-bag term in which a diverse group of writers were lumped together in the mid-20th century. They wrote about themes which advocated rebellion against traditional philosophy or against the saving graces of science and Western religion. Some of them emphasized facing squarely and bravely the dilemmas of our mortal existence while rejecting the essentialist theology of traditional Roman Catholicism. They emphasized the "absurdity" of our existence, and the value of living "authentically." The value of individual liberty in action and thought was a typical theme. Others emphasized the importance of faith in overcoming the apparent "absurdity" of our existence. After the horrors of World War 1 (heralded as the war to end all wars) were followed a few decades later by the horrors of World War 2 and the holocaust, many were looking for a new secular philosophy which would be more relevant to the radical new world which confronted the 20th century. After all, had not all sides in these wars believed that God was on their side as they continued the slaughter of tens of millions of people? Instead of bringing us the horrors of gas warfare and the atomic bomb, was science not supposed to have been the modern tool to bring heaven on earth through humane technology?

At the end of World War 2, Jean Paul Sartre called his philosophy 'existentialism', and his work, especially his plays, became well known by intellectuals and journalists. Suddenly, it seemed that elements of his philosophy could be found in other writers' works. Some of this colleagues and friends, e.g. Albert Camus, also wrote about the absurdity of being estranged from God or any Transcendent Meaning. As their themes resembled Sartre's in certain ways, they too were tagged 'existentialist', and a movement was born, or manufactured by the press and word of mouth. Manifestations of this new radical movement were popping up in music, literature, art, and architecture. If it was daring, non-religious, and depressing, it must be "existential."

Analytic philosophers in America and England considered this to be the latest trend in continental philosophy, and a few decades later, it was to evolve (or devolve) into deconstructionism. In the main, philosophers trained in the analytic tradition looked with suspicion or disdain on existentialism.

A typical reaction to existentialism might go something like this. These writers are trying to write about cosmic matters in fuzzy-minded ways. They end up saying things which are either trivial or false. They end up making recommendations that are too vague to follow or simply unworthy. For example, Sartre says we are forlorn and abandoned since belief in God is dead. This is presumptuous because it seems implausible that belief in God is dead. Where is the evidence? Second, even if such faith is a dead issue, we are not forlorn or abandoned. We still have each other and the human community. Why make such sweeping and dramatic claims? For example, Camus wrote that suicide is the only serious philosophical issue. This is incredible and silly. Philosophers, past and present, have paid attention to almost everything else but suicide. Sartre says that in choosing for ourselves, we choose for all humankind. Again, isn't this just too silly to take seriously? It may make for good dramatic effect in a novel or play, but can serious thinkers take this seriously? Writers like Sartre and Camus suggest that once we focus on our mortality and the forlorn nature of the human condition, we will be strongly motivated to take our finite existence in our own hands, to make better choices, to make the best out of our mortal death sentence. But isn't it just as likely, perhaps more likely, that we will be so depressed and overwhelmed by such thoughts that we do little or nothing, save sink into self-pity? The American philosopher, Tom Nagel, would later say that writers like Camus had been too inclined to emphasize the tragic view of the human condition. He suggested that the deeper problem was that we humans tended to take ourselves too seriously and that we ought to lighten up and consider the comic aspect of our fickle and conflicted attitudes about life.

The above points are legitimate criticisms, but I think there is much worth saving in existentialist themes. I want to take a stab at reconstituting an existentialist philosophy, based mainly on the ideas of Nietzsche, Kierkegaard, Camus, and Sartre. I do not claim my proposal to be a mirror reflection of what past "existentialist" thinkers meant to say. Rather I mean to extrapolate the themes I consider most worthy in order to build a new, and hopefully coherent, existentialist perspective. This version of existentialism will focus on the value of concrete human experience, our mortality, and the necessity of our making choices in a game whose beginning we did not choose and whose end will come whether or not we choose it. I think it will be most helpful and appealing to those who have been raised in a strict Christian, Jewish, or Muslim way, but who have had nagging doubts about the absolutes and dogma of these traditions. I am not sure I would call myself an existentialist, but depending on my mood and the day, I might feel deeply sympathetic.

This brand of existentialism will emphasize the ranking of life-versus-death issues as being of far greater importance for intellectual attention than ivory tower scholarship about issues that make little difference to human existence. This view will be more like a metaphilosophy and a lifestyle value commitment than what analytic philosophers might call "philosophy." It amounts to an attitude about human existence and how to approach doing philosophy. It ranks a philosophical or intellectual effort as less worthy if the issue(s) focused on are far from being helpful or hurtful to everyday human existence, joy, and suffering. This existentialist philosophy is one in which Socrates, Karl Marx, Buddha, Bertrand Russell, and Simone de Beauvoir could all find a home. If I am right about this, a person could affirm existentialism as an important part of his/her worldview, yet be an analytic philosopher, a philosopher of science, a Christian, a Zen Buddhist, an artist, a musician, an architect, a continental philosopher, etc. Being an existentialist will be a background metaphilosophy or metaethic which cuts across many other intellectual commitments and styles of doing philosophy.

I shall begin with a non-theist version (shared by agnostics and atheists). There are two main varieties of non-theist existentialism. One focuses on its opposition to traditional religious dogma within the Judeo-Christian-Muslim worldview. This view denies the importance of living your life according to the laws and rules allegedly laid down by an Almighty God of Judgment. The atheist believes there is no such God, and the agnostic thinks there is no compelling reason to believe in such a God, so neither of these non-believers has any reason to endorse the worldview of the Western monotheistic traditions. These existentialists focus instead on the secular world, the natural world, and the limited time we humans have on Earth to make it better or worse. They reject the essentialism of Western religion, according to which we have a human nature sculpted and defined by God's purpose for us. Religious essentialism holds that each human being has a God-given soul, that this soul is what makes us resemble God, and that we are born with a mission. That mission includes upholding God's law, multiplying and being fruitful, subduing the Earth, and having dominion over all the other creatures of the Earth. To the extent we accept and complete this mission, to that extent we are fulfilling our purpose as defined by God's plan for His creation. We are behaving "naturally." We need to learn what God's plan is (through Scripture or religious authority), then do our best (given our essential imperfectness or original sin) to act accordingly. Whether we are thought of as God's slaves, servants, or children—it is clear we are to be subservient to God. Indeed, Muslims incorporate this basic tenet into the name of their faith, 'Islam', meaning submission or surrender to God. Saying we are God's children may sound more comforting to some people's ears, but we must remember that in comparison to God the Father, we children never mature to be like our Perfect Father. Hence, we are reminded of the need for us to remain forever deferential and submissive to God.

This is an unacceptable worldview to non-theist existentialists. They must rebel against any such suggestion, which they interpret as serving the needs for power and dominance of religious authorities. (They cannot rebel against a God they do not believe exists.) These themes are played out in Sartre's *The Flies*. These existentialists think we should focus on understanding what is needed for human decency in community, promoting survival over death, and promoting happiness and respect for limits in the natural world which we shall inhabit from womb to tomb. They do not think that human beings or any particular human being is God. They do not worship SELF or HUMANITY, but they are devoted to a "down to Earth" ethic. In Christian terms, they would have to be called 'pagans' who think that human beings, while not God, are intelligent enough to know the basics of what is good and bad, fair and unfair. They think we can live morally, though not perfectly, without relying on faith in God. They reject the idea that we must choose faith in God-The-Almighty and be humble servants, or become wild and arrogant heathens believing that anything is permitted. These existentialists reject grandiose ideas that human beings have all the answers, yet they also think human beings can solve many of the problems they face. They reject both grandiosity and humiliation. As Camus suggests, they want to live with a moderate Rationality, not believing that Reason is either God or The Devil. This variety of existentialism will include many philosophers of many philosophical schools or influences, many intellectuals and artists, and many scientists.

Milton Munitz, for example, was mainly concerned to elucidate and defend philosophical naturalism, but a naturalism which recognizes a transcendent side of the natural world. He conceptualized this as "Boundless Existence." For him, this was a matter of intellectual honesty and a legitimate source of "spiritual" inspiration. He would have called himself a naturalist, not an existentialist, but his work illustrates some existentialist themes: (a) being inspired by amazement and perplexity over the world we are thrown into, and (b) human beings having the choice and responsibility for deciding how to live their existence.

> *I stress the importance of making a fundamental distinction between two principal dimensions of Reality: (1)the observable universe as the domain of interactive existents (including human*

> *existents) open to progressive inquiry, and (2) Boundless Existence, a wholly unintelligible, transcendent aspect of Reality manifested by the observable universe, though not to be confused with the common theistic conceptions of God... I propose (a) a type of humanist philosophy that assigns exclusively to human beings the choice of criteria for directing and evaluating their own lives, and (b) an intensified awareness of a level of transcendence in Reality that serves as the focus for a freshly recultivated sense of cosmic spirituality[1].*

The second variety of non-theistic existentialist is more radical in what they reject or rebel against. This type of existentialist is just as skeptical of the saving graces of modern science as of traditional Judeo-Christian-Muslim religion. Whereas many secular thinkers tend to be very optimistic about the ability of reason and science to solve all urgent, human questions or problems, this second version of existentialism does not share such faith or optimism. Indeed, these existentialists tend to see such secular optimism toward science as a quasi-religious faith, treating Science as the secular equivalent of the Vatican with the Church of Science being guided by the modern priests, namely scientists. As is true for all existentialists, these existentialists too are deeply suspicious of Dogma and unquestioned commitment to authority and worldviews.

These more radical existentialists do not reject science or reason, but neither do they think that either is the totalizing salvation for human existence. They affirm the mystery and ineffable strangeness which is found in our world. They doubt the justification for the principle of sufficient reason which holds that there is a reason or causal explanation for why everything is as it is. They are not surprised that the "clock work-mechanistic" paradigm of the universe has been largely overturned by the discoveries of atomic physics and the usefulness of quantum mechanics. These existentialists do not believe in a chaotic universe. Nor do they believe that everything in the cosmos is precisely ordered. They believe that science and reason are wonderful tools, but they want to emphasize their limits. The contemporary American philosopher, Sam Keen, is a case in point. He makes the mysterious nature of the universe something akin to the object of a spiritual devotion, and he classified himself as an agnostic concerning God.

> *All worldviews, mythologies, and ideologies, whether they are religious, secular, or spiritual, are perceptual screens through which we filter our experience. They are handles that allow us to grasp and manipulate the baffling complexity of our world. None of them can finally be verified or falsified...Taking some leap of faith is an inevitable part of the human condition...While we can never offer certain proof for the absolute truth of a worldview and philosophy of life, we can establish that it satisfies or fails to satisfy the minimal requirements of reason*[2].

> *I choose to trust the surrounding mystery out of which I emerged and into which I*

> shall disappear in death and to rest secure within the darkness of the unknowable One." (69) "The first spiritual virtue of this position is humility, the willingness to remain earthly, a creature of the humus. This odd virtue involves the commitment to live joyfully with what we can know, not to cheat, not to pretend to be able to throw a bridge over the chasm that separates us from the knowledge of the whole of Being³.

All non-theist existentialists believe that the world, including ourselves, will always be more, and sometimes less, than we expect it to be. They believe that the world, including ourselves, is bound to frustrate our desires for it to be as orderly, predictable, sane, or benevolent as we would like it to be. This gap, which Camus calls the absurd, may lie within ourselves (as a practical contradiction among our own desire and beliefs), or it may lie in the relationship between our longings and the kind of world we encounter through our experience. Camus wrote "...what is absurd is the confrontation of this irrational [world] and the wild longing for clarity whose call echoes in the human heart. The absurd depends as much on man as on the world." At bottom, it makes little difference whether this "existential frustration" is born of a human-world relation or is simply born within us. As Augustine's Christianity teaches the inevitability of original sin, and the Greeks taught the inexorability of human hubris, so too the existentialist holds the world is bound to frustrate our longing for it to make sense, especially if this means some sort of deep Cosmic or Metaphysical Sense. For non-theist existentialists, there is no answer to the question, "Why is there something rather than nothing?' For them, there is no Cosmic Plan or Divine Design, no Beginning, no End, and no ultimate First Principle. For them, we are born without our choice and we will die (unless we commit suicide) without our choosing it. We are born as mortals who must, to some extent, take the world as we find it. We can hope to improve our world, and we can make every effort to do so, but existentialists (like Hindus and Buddhists) are unable to believe in Progress, i.e. some overall and inexorable tendency of the universe (perhaps by Design) to be benevolent toward any given life form. If they act to reform society, they do so without faith there are any guarantees (or any Guarantee).

They will not believe that we can depend on any karmic principle that what goes around necessarily comes around. They will not have faith that there is any safe haven or final resting place where we can rest assured that goodness, sanity, justice, and compassion will prevail or endure. For these existentialists, being honest to themselves and to their experience is a value which trumps the all-too-human drive toward wishful thinking.

This type of existentialism excludes secular humanists who have faith that capitalism, socialism, liberalism, or science will one day prevail as the lasting salvation of humankind. They consider such convictions to be as dubious as the Christian faith that one day Jesus will come again to bring eternal heaven on Earth to all who have been loyal to "the" Christian team spirit. Putting this all together, it seems safe to say that such existentialism will never be anything close to a popular or mainstream worldview. Why then contemplate it? Why take time to examine it seriously? I will have more to say about this later, but for now, suffice it to say that we should pay attention to the few as well as to the many.

What about "theistic" existentialism? The inspiration for this kind of existential philosophy came from the 19th century Danish philosopher and Christian theologian, Kierkegaard. The central themes here are the limits of rationality and the need to transcend them through faith, the silly and fantastic nature of totalizing philosophies like that of Hegel, and the need to find the path to God through our concrete, personal experience. Here we find rebellion against an early 20th century exuberant optimism about what reason and science can accomplish. We also find an insistence that those seeking or attacking Christian faith not confuse the subjectivity of authentic faith with the objective trappings of Church traditions, institutions, and rituals.

Kierkegaard was fond of making a distinction between Christianity and Christendom, the latter being the outward and institutionalized manifestation of Christian tradition. Christendom, as contrasted with Christianity or individual Christian faith, could well be idolatrous or pagan. It could easily betray the core values of personal Christian faith.

Theistic existentialism emphasizes our mortality, the apparent absurdity of our existence, i.e. no discernible Plan, much less a benevolent one, and the frustrating irrationality and unfairness encountered in life. They emphasize our longing for the Cosmos to make sense, and the effort to have faith that (in spite of it all) there is a God who cares for us. They try to manage the leap of faith, even though their reason points away from this conclusion. It is not easy, and they may have many doubts from time to time. Still, they are committed to taking this risk, seemingly irrational from a rational perspective, in order to give hope to their deepest longings. It is this tension between their sense of reason and their heart's fondest hopes, this ongoing struggle, which gives their lives added meaning.

Having presented a taxonomy of neo-existentialism, it is time to ask, "Why bother with it?" What makes this new existentialism worthy of our consideration?

To begin with, there continues to be what Camus called a "widespread sense of the absurd" in our world. Many people, including some intellectuals and philosophers, feel that the old Western style religion is no longer meaningful to them, yet they still long for there to be more meaning to their lives than simply living and dying in this fairly short lifetime. Many also feel that social-political causes and modern science do not offer them the added sense of meaning they dearly wish for. While ultra-rationalists may simply want to tell them that they should stop seeking such transcendent meaning for human existence, it is doubtful that such an admonition will do much to change the others' hearts and minds. Human beings have always lived in cultures which encouraged them to believe in mythical stories about their origins and relation to Nature or the Eternal. Many of us just seem temperamentally "hard wired" to be discontent with living in a purely immanent, secular, and familiar world. We want to know how we fit in with the Big Picture, why people do evil, why people die, what happens to us after death, etc. What do we do when neither religion nor science offer us satisfactory answers to such questions?

As Camus suggests in his *Myth of Sisyphus*, this is where existentialism can fill a void. It can offer us a scheme for dealing with our frustrations with the world we encounter from womb to tomb. This will be an alternative to the traditional religious view of Judeo-Christianity. This alternative will serve a parallel function to the Christian view of original sin or the Jewish view of our being in an ongoing relationship with our Super Parent. I will use the Christian model as my example. Given our inherently sinful nature, i.e. we cannot help but defy God in one way or another, we will need continued effort to merit God's forgiveness. God cares about sincere efforts to repent, not so much whether we actually succeed in overcoming particular sinful behavior patterns. God is perfect, and we are not. Our defiant nature will sometimes lead us away from God and grace, but our abiding faith in the existence of a loving God will keep our eyes on the prize. We will keep trying to rehab ourselves, knowing that not even saints succeed perfectly. The individual of the faith may sometimes even doubt the existence of God or God's loving nature, but what counts, and what gives added meaning to this person's life, is the ongoing struggle to remain loyal to the theistic vision, to trust that there is such a benevolent and caring Being.

Camus suggests that the atheistic existentialist (the "absurd hero," as he calls the person) can find meaning in a parallel way, and I think this would also apply to the agnostic existentialist. Here the person wants to be faithful to his or her experience, wants to be faithful to rationality without making it an idol, to humbly recognize and accept limitations, and to take pride in human mortality and autonomy. This person wants to be true to herself or himself, to accept the bitter with the sweet, and to resist the temptation to escape from sober truth into denial and comforting delusions about the Eternal and immortality. Still, being human, they will be tempted to escape from painful experience with human injustice, cruelty, and indifference. For atheistic existentialists, they will want to remain faithful to their reasoned conviction that there is no God while agnostics will want to remain faithful to the uncertainty, ambiguity, or mystery they believe characterizes the Cosmos.

Non-theist existentialists will be tempted to escape consciousness about the human fate to grow old and decrepit, to die, and (eventually) to be forgotten. Sometimes, the anxiety may be too great, and the person will escape into drugs, work-alcoholism, sexual promiscuity, social-political crusades, even attempt being religious. This is to be expected, but being guided by their bottom-line existentialist convictions, they will see these as temptations to be fought, resisted and overcome. Even if they join a Pentecostal group, they will not completely lose sight of their view that there is no God and this maneuver is done to escape pain rather than to gain truth. Yes, we can imagine spiritual deprogramming and rehab centers for atheists gone astray. There can be a 12 step program to help them back to sobriety and to help them regain the courage and self-esteem they temporarily abandoned. The Higher Power here will be the help of others, plus the trinity of Truth, Sobriety, and Courage. A similar process can be imagined for the theistic existentialist except that here the temptation will be to idolize the Church (Church authorities, traditions, rituals and dogma) or to escape into the fantastic embrace of a rational, totalizing philosophy like Hegel's). As the struggle and tensions occur and recur throughout their lives, they will gain additional meaning for their personal lives as well as for their understanding of the human condition.

Aside from holding this view of human existence, and more importantly of their own human existence, an existentialist philosopher may be a specialist in logic, metaphysics, ethics, theory of knowledge, or the history of philosophy. I think it likely, as Camus suggests, that many existentialist philosophers will gravitate more toward more concrete value issues, hence will be more concerned with applied ethics, normative ethics, social-political philosophy, or social activism. This will be due to their desire to be honest about the priorities of human existence. There is a joke that in the Middle Ages, a serious issue among Church "scholastic" philosophers was debating how many angels could dance on the head of a pin. Meanwhile, in their surrounding world, it was heresy to maintain that the Earth was not the center of the Cosmos, doctors were bleeding sick people with leeches to cure them, and women were being tortured by the Holy Inquisition to gain their confession as witches or to purge their demons through the death of their bodies. In today's world of academic philosophy, the hallowed halls are not dominated or controlled by Church authority or dogma, but much scholarly debate is about highly abstract issues that will have little or no effect on the lives of any human being. The debate nowadays might be about how many philosophers can dance around ethical theory without saying anything relevant to real world ethical problems.

In conclusion, it may well be that my version of existentialism will be useful to a relatively small group of intellectuals. For many thoroughly secular thinkers, the ideas of God, direction from God, and the possibility of life after death are simply dead or passé issues. Likewise, they see no point in philosophers attempting to tie the meaning of our lives to faith in God or the loss of faith in God. For them, existentialism can be no more than a historical eccentricity. Still, Nietzsche wrote for the few rather than the many, for those "free spirits" most at risk of being crushed under the weight of mainstream feet. In this spirit, I imagine there are still solitary souls out there in search of a worldview which rejects both the Church of Secular Reason and the Church of the Holy Transcendent.

> *If I were a tree among trees, a cat among animals, this life would have a meaning, or rather this problem would not arise, for I should belong to this world. I should be this world to which I am now opposed by my whole consciousness and my whole*

insistence upon familiarity. This ridiculous Reason is what sets me in opposition to all creation[4].

As there are "anti-heroes" in modern films, so too we might say that these solitary individuals are in need of "anti-Meaning." For them, meaning must come in the small doses of ordinary living (of frustration, suffering and joy) set against a backdrop of rejecting Cosmic meaning and purpose. They need the tension of the contrast. They need to see human existence as a drama acted out in a world full of sound and fury and perhaps signifying nothing.

1. Munitz, Milton. *Does Life Have Meaning?* Buffalo: Prometheus Books. 1993, pp. 9-10
2. Keen, Sam. *Hymns to an Unknown God.* Bantam. 1994, p. 99
3. *Ibid*, p. 70
4. Camus, Albert. *The Myth of Sisyphus* and Other Esssays,Vintage, 1983, p. 51

More Letters from the Earth: Morality & Religion, National Insecurity, & Born in the USA

Over the years, I have written many letters to the editor of local newspapers. Most of the letters were published, but some included in this book were not. In northwestern Pennsylvania, these papers are *The Meadville Tribune*, *The Erie Times News*, *The Edinboro University Spectator*, and *The Edinboro News*. In a general way, the letters were all designed to shine light on some or another problem confronting our country. They were intended to be informative criticisms of public policy issues and the ever-present dangers of ignorance and authoritarianism. Sometimes, I suggested my own "solutions," but often I simply pointed out what seemed to be threats to justice and democracy in our nation and around the world. I have desired to point out threats to our citizenry, to speak out against demagoguery and other forms of tyranny posed by our government and extremism at home. I am proud to call myself a patriotic liberal. If my letters spread more light than darkness, if they are in any way helpful to defending our nation against creeping fascism, or if they suggest paths to strengthen the seeds of democracy and social justice—I will be well satisfied.

Long ago, Mark Twain wrote his *Letters from the Earth,* and though my title to this section is similar, I make no pretense to accomplishing Twain's wonderful irony and humor. In general, my letters are not written in a satirical vein.

ATHEISM IS NOT RELIGION

In a letter, Mr. Sargent continues to argue that secular humanism and atheism are religions. This is silly. Having faith in something or another does not qualify as a religion.

Most of us have "faith" that trees, rivers, and mountains exist. I even have "faith" that Mr. Sargent exists. Do such beliefs qualify as religious faith? Of course not.

Faith and religious faith are different, and fortunately most of us realize this. Since there are different religions and different views on what God's will is, attempting to establish any one of them as a state religion would be very divisive. Shall the State promote Hinduism, Buddhism, Taoism, Islam, Judaism, Christianity, a more primal religion, or all of the above?

How do we tell when a religious group or their sacred text expresses God's will versus the will of some human beings? The Bible's Old Testament says that children are to be executed if they curse their parents. Is this really the will of God, or an extremist human attempt to enforce respect for parents?

When people of different religious faiths set about to impose God's will on everyone, you have a recipe for civil war and intolerance. When one group succeeds in imposing their view of

God's will on the rest of us, you have a recipe for self-righteous tyranny.

NO WAR ON CHRISTMAS

Some Americans have warned us of the war being waged on Christmas. They claim there is an effort to take Jesus out of Xmas. This is both sad and silly.

There is no war except in the minds of those who are struggling with misunderstanding and paranoia. Wishing someone "Merry Christmas" has the general meaning of wishing them well during the December 25 holiday season, and I know of no one, not even ardent atheists, who take offence at this.

For many, Xmas is a time of family gathering, love, and gift giving. For others, it is a time of making money from the Xmas merchandising frenzy. For kids, it is a time of awaiting Santa's visit on Christmas eve—with visions of reindeer, sugar plums, and presents under the Christmas tree.

December 25 has not always been a day to remember Jesus of Nazareth. No one knows when Jesus was born. Prior to Christians taking over the Roman Empire, December 25 and late December were times to celebrate the winter solstice or the birth of the Persian god Mithras, the Sun god. December 25 used to be a celebration of the Sun god, not the Son of God.

According to the ancient Persian faith, Mithras was born of a virgin given the title 'Mother of God'. The God remained celibate throughout his life. Mithras urged self-control, renunciation, and resistance to sensuality for his worshippers.

The drive for wishing people "Happy Holidays" is just a drive to be inclusive. It recognizes that not all Americans are right wing, fundamentalist Christians. Most Christians simply want to live and let live. Other Americans are Jewish, Muslim, Buddhist, Hindu, American Indian, agnostic, or atheist.

Christmas is a symbol of love, compassion and generosity. Even non-Christians may want to celebrate the Christmas season in their own way.

Let our American diversity be tolerated, not stifled by a zealous minority who demand we all celebrate Xmas in the terms they dictate.

TEACHING CREATION STORIES IN SCHOOLS

What should schools and churches teach about the origin of our world? There are a number of religious stories about the creation of the world, at least 30 from around the world, including the two stories in Genesis 1-2. There is also, of course, the scientific story about the Big Bang.

Should our public schools teach the religious stories about the origin of the cosmos? They certainly can if it is done as religious studies without being an advocate for any particular religious story. Our Constitution prohibits the taking of religious oaths as a requirement for holding public office, and it also prohibits our government from establishing any religion as our State religion.

Christian reconstructionists resent the fact that a secular document like our Constitution is the supreme law of the United States. They think the Bible should be the supreme law of our land. If we are to be a nation of laws rather than forceful personalities, the ethical and lawful approach for such reconstructionists would be for them to amend our Constitution so that their version of true religion is the law of our land.

Sometimes, religious fundamentalists cast the debate over teaching evolution in our schools as a matter of fairness. "Give the religious story equal time," some say. No, this is not about fairness. These people do not want the theory of evolution given equal time in their Sunday schools or Bible study groups. They want their version of religion to be taught as the gospel truth to all our kids.

ONE GROUP SEEKS TO DOMINATE

Mr. Scarlett has written in favor of the Marriage Protection Amendment. If adopted, this amendment would deny gays and lesbians the legal right to consecrate their love within the contract of marriage. What are the author's arguments? One, "civilized cultures" have always built their societies on the foundation of heterosexual marriage.

In reply, I say the dominant culture usually believes that what is natural to its lifestyle represents all that is natural and best. In any case, civilizations, including Christendom, have often built their foundations on war, greed, racism, slavery, sexism and other forms of cruelty. Sometimes, "civilized" people rationalize such cruelty in the name of fighting heathens, pagans, witches, terrorists or evildoers. Another argument is that no one is denying gays a right to marry, because there is no constitutional right for gays to marry. This is silly. In our Constitution, there is no explicit right to any kind of marriage, period.

Each person is guaranteed the "equal protection of the laws." The legal argument in favor of gay marriage is that marriage is a matter of (deeply) personal life and liberty. Hence, denying marriage to gays is an infringement of equal protection. Another argument is that if homosexuals are allowed to marry, the very concept of marriage will lose its meaning within a short time. Of course, this is not true. Marriages will no longer be the exclusive right or privilege of heterosexuals. That would be the only change. I fear the real agenda here is for one religious culture to dictate its values to everyone else. Its adherents, of course, presume their values are God's values. What a coincidence!

GOOD GUYS ARE ABOVE THE LAW

Once again the Bush regime is trying to get our troops and government officials exempted from war crimes prosecution. Now they are working behind the scenes to get the UN Security Council to extend such an exemption to US forces around the world.

This attempt to hold the world to one standard and our side to a lesser standard must revolt all but fanatics and fascists in our own country. It is the sort of Bush foreign policy which creates more resentment and ill will towards our nation.

Let our nation's leaders cease acting as arrogant cowards. In committing our nation to a crusade against foreign evil doers, what sacrifices and what risks have President Bush, Messrs. Cheney, Rumsfeld, or Ashcroft, or Ms. Rice been willing to accept for themselves? Their personal sacrifices are almost nothing compared to those they are asking our own troops and citizens elsewhere to bear.

Enough of the attitude that our people cannot do monstrous things! You don't have to be a Muslim extremist or a foreigner to be an evildoer. The Bible says God sent the flood because people around the world had become too violent. Evil doing can be committed by people professing themselves to be Christians. An American President can sanction evil doing.

Ronald Reagan said the former Soviet Union was the focus of evil in the world. Ordinary Americans must wake up and retire George W. Bush this election year. If not, his regime will surely make our nation the focus of hatred in the world.

BUSH: THE COMPASSIONATE CONSERVATIVE?

What is a "compassionate conservative?" The current President Bush still likes to say this about himself. He borrowed the idea from his daddy, who liked to speak about the "kinder and gentler America" he favored. So, naturally, Papa Bush took us to war and became a one term President.

Does this refer simply to a conservative that has warm, fuzzy feelings about puppies, little kids, orphans, moms, dads, and apple pie? Maybe, but having the "warm fuzzies" does not tell us how they will act on this politically. After all, a liberal or the politically uninvolved can have the "warm, fuzzies."

Buddha, the Dalai Lama, and Einstein urge us to widen our circle of compassion so that it embraces more than our self, our family and relatives, our community, our nation, or even our planet. It is to include showing love and kindness to all of creation. Jesus said one of the two most important commandments is to love our "neighbor," which surely can be interpreted in a very broad manner. Earth is our human family's neighborhood. Is this what a "compassionate conservative" advocates—that we should conserve and protect all of creation? How does the Bush policy of waging aggressive war to produce regime change fit into this picture?

Would someone call himself a "compassionate conservative" simply because it is a warm, fuzzy label, the kind that might get some people to vote for you? Would the current President stoop to that tactic? Could it be a label he adopts because it makes him feel good about himself, a kind of delusional self-promotion? Who knows? Reformed drunks never give up some of their thinking habits even if they never drink again.

LET MORAL VALUES GUIDE U.S.

Our domestic and foreign policy needs to be guided by basic decency and integrity. If we cannot win by being faithful to basic moral values, we do not deserve to win.

Basic decency includes commitment to the equal value of lives everywhere, and that American lives are no more or less valuable than foreign lives. This means liberty and justice for the whole world, not just the wealthy and powerful. This means using force and violence only as means of last resort. Finally, avoid hypocrisy.

We are in the habit of judging our enemies and adversaries by focusing on the means they use and dismissing their goals. Thus, we freely label a wide range of actions as "terrorist" because people use violent means to accomplish goals in opposition to us. We are not interested in enemy goals so long as they use such violent means to attain them. On the other hand, we expect our own actions to be judged primarily on our good intentions rather than the means we use to attain our goals.

We assume American colonists were revolutionaries and rebels, not terrorists, when they used violence to gain political independence from England. The English, on the other hand, called our sons of liberty "sons of violence."

Bombing Afghanistan further into the stone age and killing thousands of civilians is justified as the unintended consequence of targeting Osama bin Laden and destroying his training camps in that nation. Invading Iraq and devastating much of that nation is justified on a variety of revolving goals. Take your pick.

The point is that we expect to be forgiven for the means we use to accomplish our goals because our goals are good. We expect our actions to be understood. We are impatient or hostile to those who suggest our enemies' actions need to be understood.

They are like demons, and we are like angels of liberty.

If ever we were to focus on comparing our goals with their goals, or enemy tactics with our own tactics, we would begin to see the world in a more balanced and honest way. As the Bush crusade against global evil doers continues, I will not hold my breath. Tens of millions of Americans are still sound asleep or living a dream which is a nightmare for most of the world.

THE DARK SIDE

A conservative U.S. Senator, Barry Goldwater, was fond of saying that "Extremism in the defense of liberty is no vice." Of course, extremists think this way, but extremism in anything is wrong and uncivilized.

Yet, President Bush and his supporters think that extremism in waging war on terrorism is justified in the name of national security. Self-defense and national defense are rational and good. Doing so with extremist measures is not rational or good.

Extremism, by definition, is an unbalanced approach, an unbalanced reaction to life's problems. Extremism in attitude usually leads to extremism in action. Extremism breeds double standards, hypocrisy and simpleton thinking.

Simpletons think their friends and loved ones should be considered innocent until proven guilty while strangers and foreigners should be considered guilty until proven innocent. Simpletons think their friends and loved ones should be judged by their good motives and intentions while strangers and foreigners should be judged by their actions.

There is indeed an ongoing struggle between the forces of good and evil in the world, but when we identify our side uniquely as the noble heroes, then those who fight against us must be thought of as villains and evildoers. We turn our cartoon inner world into a living nightmare for planet Earth. We project our dark side into the world instead of dealing with it.

The world is not neatly divided between nations of good guys and nations of bad guys. Every nation has its own share of extremists and evildoers. A modern Holy War to rid the world of evildoers will fail just as miserably as earlier holy wars because their quest is marred by a distorted view of reality. Extremist warriors fail to see the evil within themselves, and they fail to see the good in those who oppose them.

CONSISTENCY IN VALUING LIFE?

Responding to the Terry Schiavo case, we have heard many conservatives say that in cases where the facts are unclear, we should err on the side of life. This can be a very noble position if maintained consistently and not used for political opportunism.

Since we are all under a mortal death sentence, we have no absolute right to life, and I think we should temper the right to life with the right to compassion. Our life can become so miserable or hopeless that it is no longer worth living.

If we can be mistaken whether a person convicted of murder is really guilty, should we not err on the side of life? Shouldn't we eliminate the death penalty in the United States in order to err on the side of life? If we really care about protecting innocent lives, isn't the death penalty barbaric?

If we really care about protecting innocent lives and the facts are unclear about whether a nation has weapons of mass destruction and poses a grave threat to our security, should we not err on the side of life and resist going to war? In every war, we know that many innocent lives will be lost and devastated. Shouldn't we err on the side of life?

It would be great to live in a culture of life, consistently applied throughout our nation, but I fear we live in a culture of lies and make believe. We were deceived about the need for a war in Iraq. Now, the Bushies are crying wolf about the impending doom of Social Security. Our leaders condemn others in the world for violating human rights while they sanction illegal detentions and the use of torture in their crusade against terrorism.

To err on the side of life is noble, but to gag on delusion and hypocrisy is not noble.

INTELLIGENCE-BASED FAITH?

Instead of faith-based intelligence, which the Bush regime relies on heavily, we need intelligence-based faith. We need this in our national security policy, and we need it in religion-based moral codes. Instead of the attitude "Don't let the facts get in my way," we should use facts to guide our choices in life.

Here are some facts. Some people who call themselves "Christian" say we need to have a nation which follows God's laws. They sometimes say "The Constitution cannot save you," meaning that only God or Jesus leads to salvation. What is God's law? According to Jews? According to Christians? We must remember that, according to the Bible, most people have never (in any age) been good at following God's law.

The Old Testament makes clear that God sent the great flood in Noah's time because people had become too violent, not because they were engaging in gay sex. The 10 Commandments include: Thou shall not kill. In the Gospels, Jesus makes clear that we are to love our neighbor and our enemy. The most violent thing Jesus ever did was to chase the money lenders out of the temple. Would God approve of a preemptive war against a nation (Iraq) that never attacked us or threatened to attack us? What would Jesus do?

Jesus said it is easier for a camel to go through the eye of a needle than for a rich man to get into heaven. His ministry was with the poor and the outcasts of his society. Does this tell us anything about a good Christian ethic regarding the poor and welfare assistance?

The Old Testament says children are to be executed if they curse at their parents. Do fundamentalists think we should begin this practice? If we use our intelligence, does it make sense that a loving and just God would issue such a command?

For my own part, when I read in the Bible of harsh treatments of enemies, and cruel punishments, when I read about females being less important than males, I think such words come from unjust and cruel human beings. Only when I read of love and merciful justice do I detect the imprint of God.

What would Jesus do? What would Moses do? Are Christians and religious Jews prepared to follow these role models?

LET'S BE FAIR-MINDED

Recently, William Bennett, a conservative intellectual, made some remarks that were picked up and spread, without regard to their context, in a way that made Mr. Bennett look like a genocidal racist toward African-Americans. The story was mishandled by much of the media. The coverage was incompetent and morally reprehensible.

I am very liberal and a member of the Green Party, but I find this treatment of Mr. Bennett to be an example of media journalism at its worst. Mr. Bennett had engaged in a hypothetical example, in response to a caller to his radio talk show, in order to demonstrate a terrible argument for abortion, and he emphasized that the hypothetical argument was morally disgusting.

Mr. Bennett has worked most of his adult life to oppose racism in our society. He and his wife have long worked to create programs to help African-American children in poor areas escape from that poverty and become well educated. The recent portrait of Bennett in the media must have broken their hearts.

This is not a liberal versus conservative issue. All Americans who care about decency should register their voice against such character assassination in media (or anywhere). People's remarks deserve to be put in context, and they should not be given a sinister interpretation unless the evidence is overwhelming that the remarks were meant with malice.

Reporters in the media should go back to journalism 101 in order to exercise integrity in what stories they run with and how they spin those stories. Sensationalism and being the first to break a story, making audience share the bottom line, will continue to make our media look more and more like National Enquirer nonsense.

Conservatives should condemn their own when they go after liberals as if we were all in a war where everything goes. Liberals should condemn their own when they engage in such barbarism. Let basic decency and competency be the rule.

LOYALTY TO TRUTH MUST PREVAIL

Winning is a good thing, but we must also know when to let go. It is no shame not to win a war that should never have been started. Anyhow, our troops surrounded Baghdad and removed Saddam's regime from power. They won the only victory that could have been expected of them. Unity is a good thing for families and for our nation, but "United we stand" is a slogan with little meaning. The people who promote it think everything will be fabulous if only the rest of us unite behind their point of view. Of course, we can all just as well unite behind the view that the war in Iraq is wrong and must stop. They say "United we stand," but what they really want is for everyone to accept their stance on the war.

"Support the troops" is another slogan with great emotional meaning, but not much else. None of us wants harm to come to our troops anywhere in the world, but what is the best way to support them? There are many ways, short of supporting the war, to support our troops. What are we to do when the president and Congress authorize delusional and reckless military actions? Most of the nations of the world, and even our own senators, did not have the same intelligence information as President Bush did prior to the invasion of Iraq. Nor did most world leaders, the United Nations, and a huge number of Americans, think the invasion of Iraq was necessary for world or U.S. security. Bush and his vice president are once again not telling us the truth. We owe it to our troops to be more loyal to the truth than anything our politicians parade as the truth. We owe it to our troops to oppose the war policy of this president and Congress. Let's bring our troops home very soon.

RESPONSIBILITY IMPLIES BLAME

After the disaster caused by Katrina, many people have been trying to figure out why emergency aid took so long to get to the victims. They have also been trying to assess the extent to which government officials at the local, state, and federal levels bear responsibility for the slow response. When a reporter at a White House press conference kept asking questions about Bush's role in the fiasco, Bush's press secretary, Scott McClellan, repeatedly refused to comment, saying the reporter was "playing the blame game."

I was struck by how, over and over again, McClellan simply dismissed the reporter's questions as if assigning blame in political life or life in general is some kind of sinister or silly game. Bush has stated that he is ultimately responsible for any federal slowness or ineptness at getting aid to the victims of Katrina. Is it that he accepts responsibility, but not blame? What a fine example GOP apologists set for our kids by using this "blame game" rhetoric! When I tell my son he is blameworthy for not getting his homework done, or attempt in any way to assign blame to him for his behavior or attitude, he can reply to me, "Dad, you are just trying to play the blame game, and I won't play that game with you." Tricks with language cannot shield any of us, even a president, from avoiding responsibility for intentional or negligent wrongdoing. We are not ruled by a king, and even if we were, kings, too, can be responsible for wrongdoing.

THE GOLDEN RULE & COUNTING OUR BLESSINGS

The 4th of July has come and gone again. This is a day for being thankful and to celebrate our having won independence from England's King George. For many, July 4th is mainly a family day for fun, fireworks, good food, and beer.

For many, it is a day to celebrate the blessings of freedom and security which they assume we enjoy because of our military and the many soldiers who have fought or died in our wars. It is a self evident truth, an article of faith, for many Americans that our good life is largely due to our military muscle.

I pause to give thanks for our many blessings, including our large measure of liberty, but I reflect more on the basic decency by which most people here and elsewhere live their day-to-day lives. I notice that the great majority of people are not driven by greed, selfishness, or hatred in their everyday lives. Neither do they choose violence as a means to get what they want or settle their conflicts. I notice that most kids are raised by parents who love them, show that love to them, and try their best to be responsible parents. Their parents teach them not to be selfish or greedy, and not to resort to violence except in self defense.

How much our blessings of security and liberty depend on our being a military Superpower in the world is a highly debatable issue. After all, we were this military Superpower on 9-11, but this did not prevent fanatics from killing nearly 3000 people in their attacks on NYC and the Pentagon. After all, we were far from being a Superpower when we defeated the world's reigning Superpower of the 18th century, England.

I think we can be thankful that in our country and around the world, the norm is for people to treat each other with basic decency and respect. The norm is for people to treat their neighbor as they would want to be treated. War and violence are not rare. They are hideously present in the world, but they are not the norm. Be thankful that our blessings of liberty and security are usually protected not by police, armies, and weapons, but are kept safe instead by the ordinary decency of ordinary people.

PEACE & JUSTICE CENTER PROUD OF 'LOVING MESSAGES'

Recently, Mr. Pontzer wrote expressing his views that "God bless the whole world" is really just about hating America and slamming "God bless America." His letter shows how extremist some folks are in their mixing of religion and politics. He says it is just about asking that we pay special attention to the nation that guards our security and freedom. I guess this is what German patriots felt in World War II as they went into battle with "God is with us" on their belt buckles. It has been absolutely the norm for every nation, especially in wartime, to want to think that God is on their side. America is special, very special, but it is not so special that God would care only to bless our nation and not all of God's creation. The point of the "God bless the whole world" message is to remind people that the God of the Old and New Testament cares about people everywhere. Just as Pontzer says that "God bless America" does not mean that we are trying to take anything away from people in other nations, so too "God bless the whole world" does not mean we are trying to take anything away from Americans. The Erie Peace and Justice Center is proud to have sponsored loving messages in our community, including billboards with the "God bless the whole world" message. Pontzer will find that most Catholic and Episcopal churches in our area have embraced this message. "God bless the whole world" is not about hating America. It is about the need for loving the world. Rightwingers need to wake up and figure out that just because many of us are vehemently opposed to their politics, this does not mean we hate our country. Love of country does not translate into "Thou shalt love ultraconservative political views." God is not Democrat or Republican, liberal or conservative, Christian or Muslim, American or non-American. Our ultraconservative citizens need to stop trying to wrap themselves in God's blessing. Their views and actions can just as well damn as save them.

U.S. POLICY SHOULD BE 'FAIR TRADE' OVER 'FREE TRADE'

As a nation, we should favor fair trade, not free trade, and a living wage, not a minimum wage. Fair trade means that the bottom line goes beyond profits, market share, and jobs. Fair trade extends to protecting our nation's sovereignty, the environment and workers rights. Under NAFTA, panels of judges chosen by government and business interests are the final arbiters of trade disputes between Canada, Mexico and the United States. These panels operate in secret and issue decisions when a foreign corporation claims (under Chapter 11 of the agreement) their profits have been hurt by a local labor, fair practice or environmental regulation. Their decisions trump even our U.S. Supreme Court. The state of California, for example, was challenged by a Canadian corporation who made a hazardous additive for gasoline. When California realized this hazardous chemical was polluting drinking water, they banned it. Under Chapter 11 of NAFTA, the Canadian chemical firm argued

California must halt the ban or pay them for lost profits, arguing the ban is "tantamount to expropriation" of their product.

Without labor, human rights and environmental protection, "free trade" agreements are really fast-track agreements for greed and special business interests. Every nation ought to be allowed to protect labor, human rights and the environment. Fortunately, there are international standards for doing this, Universal Declarations on Human Rights, arranged by the United Nations and signed by most nations. As for minimum-wage jobs, these wages are not now (nor have they ever been) nearly enough to keep a person out of poverty. Jobs should all pay high enough wages to keep an employee above the poverty line as defined by the federal government, and part-time jobs should pay the same hourly wage. This is basic decency. Having a decent job is not a privilege, but a right for anyone with the qualifications and will to do the work. If some owners of companies would rather go out of business than pay living wages to their employees, if they would rather relocate to other nations where the labor costs are dirt cheap — so be it! Such owners are unpatriotic, but they are free to go. Let them pay a "severance" fee for the hardship caused here by their selfish behavior, and let them consider this a part of the cost of doing business in the U.S. There is a price to be paid for protecting fair trade and fair labor, and all citizens should be ready to pay it.

SAVING SOCIAL SECURITY OR DESTROYING IT?

For those who have no care for history, let me point out that George W. Bush has been claiming that Social Security is bankrupt since 1978. From the time SS became law in 1935 until the present, certain conservatives have railed against it, claiming it would not work or, worse yet, it is socialism.

Let's talk straight about SS. It is an insurance plan and, from time to time, it has problems that need to be addressed. The amount of money needed to cover full benefits for all recipients past the year 2042 can be gotten by raising payroll taxes, ending the cap on paying SS taxes (so that all taxpayers, even the very wealthy, pay into the system), ending benefits for high income taxpayers (say $500,000 or above), reducing our national debt, Bush budget deficits, or pumping emergency funds into SS from general revenue funds. An improved economy where more good jobs are created would also be of great help because there would be more payroll tax money pumped into SS.

Some conservatives now oppose (and have from the beginning opposed) SS because it is a successfully operated government program with control over vast amounts of citizen dollars that private business interests cannot get their hands on. It shows that tax revenues can be used efficiently and productively to serve our citizenry, to help keep our people out of poverty in their elder years. This they loathe because they are fanatical, true believers who worship at the shrine of Capitalism.

These ultra-conservatives think that private enterprise should be the only efficient and healthy way to meet society's needs. With a few exceptions like the armed forces and police, these folks bow down before the god of private enterprise. Don't bother them with the facts; they have sworn their heart and mind's allegiance to their "God of mammon."

There is no current crisis in SS, and its future potential problem of being short in its funding pool cannot be helped by siphoning money away into private investment schemes. Can we shore up the SS general fund by reducing it? Duh?

DEFINING TORTURE

Recently, allegations of the CIA torturing prisoners have been in the news. While pundits, TV anchors, and government officials wonder aloud whether harsh interrogation methods like "water boarding" count as torture, we might just take a look at what the law says about "torture."

Here is what the Convention against Torture (which became our U.S. law in 1994) says.

"For the purposes of this Convention, the term "torture" means any act by which severe pain or suffering, whether physical or mental, is intentionally inflicted on a person for such purposes as obtaining from him or a third person information or a confession, punishing him for an act he or a third person has committed or is suspected of having committed, or intimidating or coercing him or a third person, or for any reason based on discrimination of any kind, when such pain or suffering is inflicted by or at the instigation of or with the consent or acquiescence of a public official or other person acting in an official capacity." (Article I, 1)

I hope this helps those of us who have difficulty defining `is', `sex with that woman', and other efforts to avoid personal accountability for criminal violations. Let's hope we haven't lost all our humanity and sanity after 9-11.

JUSTICE FOR ALL

When we say our Pledge of Allegiance, we pledge to be a nation "with liberty and justice for all." Our Constitution states that a guiding purpose of "We the People" is to "establish justice" and "provide for the common welfare."

Are these just pretty words to make us feel good?

When it comes to economic justice, hasn't our nation has always been deaf to justice for all? Business interests complain about raising the minimum wage, and they try to block such raises.

Shouldn't every person who is willing and able to work deserve a "minimum" wage? Don't they deserve more than this, namely a living wage to keep them above the poverty line? Shouldn't every employee receive an annual cost of living adjustment (COLA) to keep pace with the increased costs of living?

Most business interests say no to COLA, oppose efforts to raise the minimum wage, and oppose any mandate to pay employees a living wage. They say such changes will actually harm workers because inflation will be fueled and business owners will have to lay off some workers or go out of business.

But, to establish justice and provide for the common welfare, isn't this precisely where government should be ready and able to help out displaced workers? Yet, this too is staunchly opposed by many because they say we must have less, not more, government.

Most people are not paid well enough for the jobs they do, and there are not enough good jobs to go around. People feel insecure and envious of others who have more than they do.

Free trade agreements and globalization make them fear losing their jobs. It keeps most working people divided against one another.

There is no class warfare in the United States, just minor skirmishes between some employees and their bosses. As the prophet, George Orwell wrote of the "proles" in his 1984 story, most people will accept their lot in life so long as they have enough money or credit to buy their toys, drink some beer, gamble, and play hard on the weekends.

THE MORALITY OF CIVIL DISOBEDIENCE

Recently, a person wrote that the Erie 9 war protesters, who committed non-violent acts of civil disobedience, are taking the first steps toward anarchy and that unless we all obey the laws, our civilization begins to fail. The bottom line, for that writer, seems to be that no one should knowingly break any law, lest we slide into chaos.

I would remind people with such views that our nation was born in protest, law-breaking, and eventually violent revolution against King George. The Sons of Liberty regularly dragged collaborators with England out of their homes, burned the houses down, and beat up those they judged to be collaborators with King George.

I would also remind people that the Erie 9 acted in the same respect for civil law that inspired Gandhi and Martin Luther King Jr. to resist injustice. These fine Erie-area citizens did no violence, and they accepted personal responsibility for their actions by going to jail or paying fines. These are hardly the actions of anarchists.

Finally, what is a citizen to do when the President and Vice President break the law and dishonor their vow to uphold and protect the Constitution? This they have done in too many ways to detail in this letter, and so far, neither lawbreaker has been held accountable.

Bush and Cheney have done their part in undermining respect for law and moral decency, to say nothing of crippling our nation's credibility with nearly the whole world. If our civilization is failing, surely a great cause of this is that our "leaders" themselves are arrogant law-breakers, hence bad examples to our children and the civilized world.

FASCISM IN AMERICA

The American Legion (with 2.7 million members) has recently declared that there should be no more public protests against the war in Iraq. They say protesters should simply write letters to Congress or President Bush. At a recent convention in Hawaii, they voted to use whatever means are necessary to "ensure the united backing of the American people to support our troops and the global war on terrorism."

We live in a flawed democracy, but it is one worth protecting and enhancing. The price of our freedom is eternal vigilance, for democracy can be frittered away and lost. It can easily be lost as citizens give more and more power to central government, usually out of fear of enemies abroad and at home.

This is how the fledgling German democracy of the 1930s was lost. Hitler's fascist party rose to power within the democratic process, and Hitler was elected to their parliament. As Germans suffered more and more from the worldwide depression, and Hitler pledged to protect them from Middle Eastern terrorists (then it was Jews not Muslims), ordinary German citizens were ready for his strong man leadership when he seized absolute power. Ordinary Germans embraced Hitler's assertion that Germans were an exceptional people, meant to fulfill their destiny as world rulers.

People think that "fascism" is all about Hitler and Mussolini, but fascism goes way beyond those two historical examples of fascism. The Roman Empire was the inspiration for the very creation of this political philosophy. Fascism refers to the movement's emblem, the fasces, a bundle of rods bound around a projecting axehead that was carried before an ancient

Roman magistrate by an attendant as a symbol of authority and power.

Fascism is all about authoritarian or dictatorial society in which opposition is censored or forcibly suppressed, a society guided by the belief that their people and culture are superior to other nations. Fascists believe that the lives of "their people" (because they are exceptional) are more worthy than those of inferior peoples.

Apparently, the Legionnaires simply dismiss our first amendment right to peaceably assemble and to petition our government to remedy grievances we have with government behavior. No doubt some of them are completely unaware of this Constitutional right we have as citizens of this republic.

During the old Cold War and under the Bush War on Terrorism, rightwing extremists feel free to spew their fascism in the name of patriotism. Shame on them, and shame on us if we allow them to destroy our democracy with their brutal and simpleton approach to the complex, real problems we face.

APOCALPSO?

As rapid global warming continues to wreak uncontrollable havoc on human lifestyles and the global economy, as the Pied Pipers of industrial prosperity continue to sing their sentimental Ra-Ra songs, and as the American

Empire continues to overreach and spread thin its military resources, common people will become more marginalized, victimized, and angry.

Where will they turn to vent their indignation and rage? What armies of private security guards will protect the smug, gated communities against the chaos created by their greed and denial?

Disease, vendettas, and brutal survival struggles are in the wings.

Who will give comfort and shine light on the new Dark Age sprinting to our front lawns and doorsteps? Will everyone plead "Not guilty" and "I don't recall" when the new prosecutors come to call?

I pose this parable and riddle to all those who still can hear and see the consequences of our current politics and value system.

JESUS AND CAPITALISM

As reported on TV news this morning, the gap between the rich and the rest of us in this country continues to grow. According to the news report, the annual income of the wealthiest 1% is now 400 times greater than the great majority of income earners in our the United States. If we were to factor in assets from property owned, this gap increases even more dramatically.

One electronic chain store is laying off most of its long term and skilled workers, but offering them a chance to reapply for lower pay doing the same jobs. This outrage is the price of unrestrained capitalism and greed. "Globalization" is just a code word for "what's good for big business is good for the whole planet."

Under the Bush regime, with their tax cuts for the wealthy and their borrow-and-spend plan to pay for perpetual war against evildoers, we are a nation reeling under record national debt and a declining quality of life for most Americans. Our middle class is shrinking, our poor are growing poorer, and we have a President who claims he is a born again Christian.

Taxes will have to be raised in the not-too-distant future to pay for the money Bush has borrowed to pay for his global crusade, and this tax burden will fall on ordinary working Americans. The network of social services and safety net so important to most Americans will have to shrink in order to pay off the costs of war and corporate welfare.

Jesus spent his ministry (Luke 4:18) healing and serving the poor and outcasts of society. He preached (Mark 10:17-25) that it would be extremely difficult for the rich person to enter the kingdom of heaven. Jesus explicitly rejected (Matthew 5:38-9) the old "eye for an eye" in favor of nearly total pacifism.

Candidate Bush once said that Jesus was his favorite "political" philosopher because Jesus changed his life. I wonder if Jesus would ask George W. Bush, "And why do you call me, Lord, Lord, and do not the things which I say?" (Luke 6:46)

THE WISDOM OF HAMLET

Wisdom in every age has been in short supply. What passes for wisdom, on the other hand, is readily available to all of us. VIPs and opinion leaders lead us in chants to the tune of "common sense." It is odd that normally what is rare, rather than the common, is what has high value, and yet "common sense" is presumed to be of great value.

Here are several examples of this oddity. Common sense, folk wisdom says "He who hesitates is lost," yet also maintains "Haste makes waste." Established modern "common sense" maintains that "socialism" is evil, yet also that it is good to be social and good to have a social conscience. The opposite of being social is being antisocial or selfish, yet we are taught that "socialism" is very bad. Go figure!

Our state and national parks are socialist institutions, and so are Social Security, Medicare, Medicaid, public education, and our Armed Forces. Does wisdom tell us that these "socialist" institutions are evil? Is this the verdict of "common sense?"

Do you ever wonder whether "life is a tale told by an Idiot, full of sound and fury, signifying nothing?' Are our hearts and minds filled with propaganda and nonsense, and if so, who fills us up with such hogwash? Who are the wolves in sheep's clothing?

SCHOOL ASSESSMENT TESTS ARE NOT HELPFUL

I was moved by the letter from a student at East High concerning the PSSA assessment tests. The idea was that traditional methods of assessing students' progress (grades on report cards) were inadequate. The idea was that lazy or incompetent teachers were inflating grades, and lots of students were graduating high school who couldn't read, write, or do math. Public schools and their teachers needed to be held accountable.

No matter what method of assessment is employed, students can graduate high school and not be good at reading, writing or math. There is no magic bullet, and punishing schools for the failure of some students is a harsh and stupid approach to educational problems. In any case, this approach is prejudiced against public schools, since private and religious schools need not meet these severe standards. If we want to improve student learning, we need to take well-known steps. To begin with, if parents are not able or willing to work with schools to help their kids do well in school, the teachers can do little. Do we need assessment penalties for parents whose kids do poorly, say paying higher taxes if their kids do poorly on the PSSA test? Poorer school districts need more money to provide their students an equal opportunity to succeed. Class sizes need to remain small, so that students can receive more individual attention.

HAMPLE DOES STATE'S BIDDING

Several people have written letters recently criticizing the pay raises received by Judith Hample, chancellor of the State System of Higher Education. After all, State System teachers were told to forgo even cost-of-living increases. They were told they had to pay more for their health insurance. As a result of the state continuing to cut support for the 14 state schools (a trend for more than 20 years), tuition continues to rise while the number of faculty continues to shrink. Students or their parents have to pay more for larger classes taught by fewer professors. Who mainly suffers from political decisions to continually cut back funding? Yes, low-income and middle-class families. With current trends in Pennsylvania's Legislature and governor's office, we can kiss goodbye the ideal of higher education of all Pennsylvanians. No one should be surprised by the huge salary and benefits awarded Hample. It is not about fairness. Our state politicians are more than happy to pay one CEO so she can reduce the salaries and benefits of thousands of teachers. Who needs public higher education, anyway? Not the wealthy. It was instituted for the poor and the middle class. Churches can have more soup kitchens for those who cannot make it on temp jobs that pay minimum wage with no benefits. Wealthy folks and private enterprise fanatics can then point out this is merely survival of the fittest. They can bemoan the inclination to crime and laziness among the "undesirable elements" of society.

Thank God there is no such thing as class warfare.

SCAPEGOATING SMOKERS

In a recent editorial, your paper argued that Pennsylvania should join other states in banning smoking in all public places. In your editorial, you said "Smoking and smokers are driving up health-care costs for every American. Smoking not only makes you sick, but it's also often a killer."

The real health risks of smoking are well-established, and there can be reasonable bans on where people can smoke, but there are also well-established health risks from a wide variety of sources we accept as facts of life. If anti-smoking zealots really care about protecting the health of our public, they should likewise urge bans on public exposure to toxins from heavy industry, cars, buses, trucks, vans, SUVs, and fossil fuel energy plants. The public is also involuntarily exposed to those threats, and in a much more massive and daily way. Such prolonged exposure is "often a killer."

Never mind polluting our environment with industrial products and by-products like pesticides and PCBs. The stacks of industry and our fossil fuel cars contribute greatly to ozone clouds hanging over our urban areas. These cause and exaggerate respiratory illnesses like emphysema. Our rivers, lakes, and oceans are dumping grounds for "farm run off" and industrial poisons like dioxin.

Our society has given new meaning to "nuclear family" due to decades of nuclear fallout from above ground atomic bomb testing, radioactive waste from the civilian and defense industry, radioactive smoke detectors that end up in landfills, etc. This exposure also shortens people's lives and inflates health care costs for all of us.

To target only smoking in public places is arbitrary and leaves most public health risks untouched. To begin to heal our toxic society, we will all need to be seriously inconvenienced. We will all need to make personal sacrifices and share the pain if we are to withdraw from the poisoned society on which we have become addicted.

Smokers have become a convenient scapegoat for a society which cannot live without its poisons.

PRAYING IS NOT PERSECUTED

From occasional letters to your paper, it seems some people are convinced there is a ban on using the word `Christ' or saying `Merry Xmas' in the public schools. This is not true. Furthermore, probably most of the teachers and staff of our public schools would identify themselves as Christians.

Neither is it true that prayer is banned in public schools. Students are free to pray to God, Allah, Jesus, Krishna, or whomever, so long as the prayer is not disruptive of class or coercive of other students. What is not allowed is for a teacher or a student to lead a prayer in class on behalf of Jesus, God, Allah, Krishna, or whatever deity.

Jesus said "when you pray, go into your inner room, close your door and pray to your Father who is in secret, and your Father who sees what is done in secret will reward you." (Matthew 6: 6). Some members of Christendom seem to have missed that teaching from the Gospels.

Some people think there was a "good old days" when the majority ruled in democracy. There were no such days.

At the founding of our nation, the law did not permit the majority of voting-age adults to vote. Women, blacks, Indians, and adult males without property (land or businesses) were excluded. A minority of white males ruled. In ancient Athens, the alleged birthplace of "democracy," women were excluded from the vote. Ancient Athens and the USA used lots of slaves to drive their economies.

In the history of Christendom, the Church has seldom been pleased to endorse democracy, believing instead that Church authorities where part of God's hierarchical plan for ruling on Earth as it is in heaven. This spiritual organizational chart brought us the Dark Ages, several crusades, the Holy Inquisition, lots of witch hunts, and mass murder.

So much for the "good old days" of majority rule.

BUSH SPEAKS LIKE WARMONGER

Poor George W. Bush is again asserting that Iran is the biggest State sponsor of terrorism around the world. Our war president is at it again. He just can't get enough. Talking tough and being tough are very different, and being a person of good judgment about the facts is not on this president's résumé.

What exactly makes Iran such a gigantic sponsor of terrorism? Has it used nuclear weapons to bomb civilians in cities, murdering 200,000? Has it sponsored the overthrow of democratic governments in Guatemala, Iran and Chile? Has it planned to assassinate foreign heads of state, say, in Cuba or Chile?

Oops, I guess this sort of barbaric behavior was sponsored by the heads of state of a different government.

Has Iran invaded another Middle Eastern nation under false pretenses to remove that nation's leader and institute a puppet government favorable to its perceived national interests? Has it stockpiled the largest and most sophisticated cache of ready-to-use weapons of mass destruction in the world? Oops, I guess that has been done by another government closer to home.

How sad we have to put up with Bush for another year. Wouldn't we all be safer if Bush and his pal, Dick Cheney, were locked away safely in prison or in a home for the bewildered?

SUPPORT THE TROOPS

Some conservatives have a mantra about the war in Iraq which they urge on the rest of us. They say, "Support the troops," no matter how you feel about the war being justified or not.

Many Americans have the car stickers with the same message.

I want to know what is meant by "Support the Troops." If I say, I do, does this mean I should accept the war and not criticize it or protest it in public? What if I believe the war is unjust and criminal?

What if my support of the troops means I want them brought home promptly? What if I don't want them further damaging international security and being placed needlessly in harms' way in a reckless mission initiated by an ill-informed and fanatical President? I definitely want our troops to return home safely. Is this an acceptable way to support our troops?

Does "supporting our troops," for Bush supporters, mean they will volunteer to serve in the armed forces so supporters can really help win the Bush war? Does it mean, if they are too old, that they will urge their kids or grandkids to enlist soon so they can go fight in Iraq? Does it mean they are willing to pay higher taxes or have their kids and grandkids pay for the tremendous borrowing done by Bush to finance the war? What sacrifices are the war supporters prepared to make in their personal lives?

I believe our troops should be used to protect our nation from attack, to protect our liberty and security. Alas, this war does not serve that purpose, but only causes death, misery and instability throughout Iraq now, and much more national and international insecurity for the future.

We should be beefing up our Coast Guard and border patrols, not sending in the Marines for "mission impossible" situations. As for those who say we must show support for our troops, if all this means is that people place a little sticker on their car, I think our troops can do without that kind of support.

ETHNIC PROFILING IS STUPID

Some Americans think that ethnic profiling, if done to protect us from terrorism, is only sensible. Be on the lookout, they say, for anyone on or around commercial jet flights who looks like they are an Arab or Muslim from the Middle East. Remember 9-11, and remember the earlier attacks on the World Trade Center in 1993.

If it looks like a duck and quacks like a duck, it probably is a duck. Sure there are exceptions, they say, but it is better safe than sorry. We have to focus on the main threat, which they see as coming from the Middle East.

Guess what? This sort of simplistic profiling not only unfairly discriminates against innocent "Muslim-looking" people, it does not work. While preparing for 9-11, the 19 suicide terrorists, in order not to be detected, shaved off their beards and avoided behaving like a Western stereotype of an Islamic radical. It worked.

Actually, there is a wide spectrum of terrorist looks and behaviors. Remember the bombing of the Federal Bldg in Oklahoma City, the bombing at the Atlanta Olympic Park, the years of terrorist acts of the Unabomber, various bombings and shootings at abortion clinics, the two African-Americans who terrorized the D.C. area, and the fellow who shot at drivers (killing one) in the Columbus, OH area.

What profile would we need for these terrorists? They are mostly white men with a sprinkling of blacks. Are our police supposed to detain or arrest anyone who looks like a white (redneck) Christian or any blacks they see boarding planes?

I hope not, but ethnic profiling, if done consistently, would point us in that nutty direction. I only hope that the fear, anger, and prejudice that still grips many Americans will not push us further into a Democrazy ruled by hatred and stupidity.

BUSH ALSO WRONG ABOUT ARAFAT

For those who have ears for history, let them hear. It was the repeated position of the Bush administration and the extremist government of Israel that Yasser Arafat stood in the way of peace between Israel and the Palestinians. There could be no progress or real negotiations so long as Arafat was the Palestinian leader. Now Arafat is gone, and all hell is breaking loose between Israel and Palestinian militants.

At the time, many of us who knew the history of the Palestine Liberation Organization and other Palestinian political organizations thought to ourselves, "Be careful what you wish for."

We knew that Arafat and the PLO had pledged under the Oslo accords to recognize the existence of Israel and were willing to compromise land for peace—and that other more militant groups were waiting in the wings.

Hamas was the natural organization to gain power when the PLO lost power. Did Bush know this? Did Israel's Likud party know this?

Are our leaders informed and rational? If so, are they being honest with us about their foreign policy in the Middle East and elsewhere?

I have to conclude on the basis of the available evidence that the real meaning of WMD is government Weapons of Mass Deception.

DENIAL AND DELUSION OPEN THE GATES OF HELL

George W. Bush and many Americans live in a cartoon fantasy life of denial and delusion. The latest National Defense Estimate gives three scenarios for Iraq now and in the foreseeable future, all grim and none involving democracy or stability. A White House spokesman has responded that this estimate is simply the pessimistic result of nay-sayers. Yet it was exactly this National Intelligence Estimate from several years ago that George W. Bush used to prove our need to invade Iraq.

After the first Gulf War led by Papa Bush, Iraq was left in shambles. Saddam's army and hapless airforce were decimated. Iraq was carved up into three zones by the Brits and our gov't, and Saddam's airforce was not permitted to fly over the northern or southern third of his own country. Severe sanctions kept his nation weak with hundreds of thousands of children dying due to lack of clean water and medical supplies. A new hero to many Muslims, Osama bin Laden, was calling Saddam an infidel. As our own intelligence community later testified and the 9-11 Commission concluded, there was no connection between Saddam and the attacks of 9-11 or international terrorism.

Saddam had no ability to threaten or attack the United States, Europe, or any of his neighbors, especially Israel. Even if he had somehow attacked Israel, he knew the Israeli retaliation would have been swift and overwhelming. He was a beaten man.

Still, George W. Bush convinced the Senate and most Americans that Saddam was a grave threat to world security because he had stockpiled nuclear, biological and chemical weapons of mass destruction. He said the UN inspectors were not competent to locate these weapons. He convinced most Americans that we needed to go to war against Saddam, to avoid a mushroom cloud over one of our cities.

No weapons of mass destruction have been found, and no credible source thinks they will ever be found. He was able to do this because most Americans don't keep informed about world events, and Senators do not want to appear weak on national security.

George W. Bush has a simple, don't-bother-me-with-the-facts approach to world affairs. Now that he and his fanatical supporters have opened up the gates of hell in the Middle East, the world will be far more brutal and insecure for generations to come.

LOYALTY TO TRUTH MUST PREVAIL

Winning is a good thing, but we must also know when to let go. It is no shame not to win a war that should never have been started. Anyhow, our troops surrounded Baghdad and removed Saddam's regime from power. They won the only victory that could have been expected of them.

Unity is a good thing for families and for our nation, but "United we stand" is a slogan with little meaning. The people who promote it think everything will be fabulous if only the rest of us unite behind their point of view. Of course, we can all just as well unite behind the view that the war in Iraq is wrong and must stop. They say

"United we stand," but what they really want is for everyone to accept their stance on the war.

"Support the troops" is another slogan with great emotional meaning, but not much else. None of us wants harm to come to our troops anywhere in the world, but what is the best way to support them? There are many ways, short of supporting the war, to support our troops.

What are we to do when the president and Congress authorize delusional and reckless military actions? Most of the nations of the world, and even our own senators, did not have the same intelligence information as President Bush did prior to the invasion of Iraq. Nor did most world leaders, the United Nations, and a huge number of Americans, think the invasion of Iraq was necessary for world or U.S. security. Bush and his vice president are once again not telling us the truth.

We owe it to our troops to be more loyal to the truth than anything our politicians parade as the truth. We owe it to our troops to oppose the war policy of this president and Congress. Let's bring our troops home very soon.

WHITE HOUSE NEWSPEAK: THE BLAME GAME

Following the human disaster caused by Katrina, many people have been trying to figure out why emergency aid took so long to get to the victims. They have also been trying to assess the extent to which different government officials at the local, state, and federal levels bear responsibility for the slow response.

When a reporter at a White House press conference kept asking questions about Bush's role in the fiasco, his press secretary, Scott McClellan, repeatedly refused to comment, saying the reporter was "playing the blame game." I was struck by how, over and over again, Mr. McClellan simply dismissed the reporter's questions as if assigning blame in political life, or life, in general is some kind of sinister or silly game. President Bush has stated that he is ultimately responsible for any federal slowness or ineptness at getting aid to the victims of Katrina. Is it that he accepts "responsibility," but not blame?

I thought this seemed strange given how eager the majority of Republicans were in Congress to blame President Clinton for his lying to the nation about cheating on his wife with Monica. They even tried very hard to find evidence to blame the Clintons for massive financial fraud, witness intimidation, sexual assault and murder. Why was the blame game right then, but wrong now? What a puzzle!

What a "fine" example GOP apologists set for our kids by using this "blame game" rhetoric! When I tell my son he is blameworthy for not getting his homework done, or attempt in any way to assign blame to him for his behavior or attitude, he can reply to me, "Dad, you are just trying to play the blame game, and I won't play that game with you."

Our actions in life can bring us moral praise or moral blame, and our system of moral checks and balances rests upon individuals learning to accept personal responsibility for their role in wrongdoing. I thought this was part of the GOP basic faith and that they distrusted liberals because they thought liberals wanted to excuse all wrongdoing as caused by factors beyond our control. I guess we have a new breed of Republicans in the Oval Office.

Tricks with language cannot shield any of us, even a President, from avoiding responsibility for intentional or negligent wrongdoing. We are not ruled by a King, and even if we were, kings too can be responsible for wrongdoing.

A-BOMBS DROPPED ON JAPAN 1945

August 6 and 9 mark the 60th anniversary of the atomic bombing of Hiroshima and Nagasaki by Harry Truman. Many in this country saw this as a justified and fitting end to a war with Japan which Japan started by the bombing of Pearl Harbor. Many still feel this way.

These bombings, which killed over 200,000 men, women and children were done intentionally. The mass civilians killed were not "collateral damage." The moral responsibility for these murders lies with the late President Truman, those who carried out his orders, and all Americans who condoned this mass slaughter.

The only attempt to give the bombings some sort of intelligent justification has been to say that if not for the bombings, more Americans and even Japanese lives would have been lost. An appeal is sometimes made to a discredited Pentagon estimate of a million more war deaths had Truman not ordered the atomic bombing.

These justifications rest on the premise that only an unconditional surrender from Japan was acceptable. This is, of course, extremist thinking spawned and nurtured by the fear and hatred of war.

The two atomic bombings at the end of the war were war crimes, and acts which showed the rest of the world that American leaders were willing to intentionally mass murder civilian populations in wartime in order to terrorize the enemy into capitulation, in order to win decisively, in order to spare the loss of our own troops. This showed the world what our government considered acceptable behavior. What do you think Osama bin Laden learned from this?

This is not blaming America. This is blaming Harry Truman and all rightwing extremists who supported the decision to commit this hideous action in 1945. Seldom do the actions of the

Congress or President (whether Republican or Democrat) represent my values or views. I think many of our present and past government officials should be in jail or exiled from the U.S.A.

BUSH TEAM ARE WAR CRIMINALS

At present, there is controversy over whether President Bush violated the law by authorizing data mining and surveillance of Americans without bothering to get court authorization (even after the fact). In February, the U.S. Senate will hold hearings to determine if Bush and his team did anything unethical or illegal. Some defend Bush by asserting that in war time, any President has this authority as the Commander in Chief, so long as it is done with the aim of protecting us from harm. I, on the other hand, say the road to hell is paved with good intentions, and this is just one more reckless and arrogant action by a White House guilty of violating U.S. and international law.

Some Americans despise the United Nations and international law, fearing it will tie our hands or lead to an evil One World Government. Our founding fathers, however, incorporated respect for international law into our Constitution, making it our duty to honor any treaty signed and ratified by our President and Congress. Article VI says:

All Treaties made, or which shall be made, under the Authority of the United States, shall be the supreme Law of the Land; and the Judges in every State shall be bound thereby, any Thing in the Constitution or Laws of any State to the Contrary notwithstanding.

Our President is obligated (Article II):

to the best of my Ability, preserve, protect and defend the Constitution of the United States.

President Bush is not King George, and must show restraint even in a war he has declared without a Congressional declaration of War (the prerogative of Congress). President Bush can and must fulfill his duties as Commander in Chief of the Armed Forces without presuming an inherent authority to do whatever he pleases in pursuit of a Terminator vision of national security. Those who think he has such authority are, in effect, endorsing fascism.

The Bush Team and high ranking military officers have probably violated the following treaties signed and ratified by our government:

- UN Charter, Article Chapters I and VII, not allowing war for the purpose of regime change
- Geneva Conventions of 1949 and 1977.

For example, the Geneva Protocol of 1977 (II, Article 4) says:

The following acts are and shall remain prohibited at any time and in any place whatsoever, whether committed by civilian or by military agents:

(a) violence to the life, health, or physical or mental well-being of persons, in particular:

(i) murder

(ii) torture of all kinds, whether physical or mental

a(iii) corporal punishment

b(iv) mutilation

(b) outrages upon personal dignity, in particular humiliating and degrading treatment, enforced prostitution and any form of indecent assault;

(c) the taking of hostages;

(d) collective punishments

(e) threats to commit any of the foregoing acts

The Bush team and high ranking military officers have probably also violated the U.S. War Crimes Act (last amended in 1996). For example:

(a) Whoever, whether inside or outside the United States, commits a war crime, in any of the circumstances described in subsection (b), shall be fined under this title or imprisoned for life or any term of years, or both, and if death results to the victim, shall also be subject to the penalty of death. The circumstances referred to in subsection (a) are that the person committing such breach or the victim of such war crime is a member of the Armed Forces of the United States or a national of the United States. The term `war crime' means any conduct (1) defined as a grave breach in any of the international conventions signed at Geneva 12 August 1949, or any protocol to such convention to which the United States is a party.

Yes, Martha, President Bush and his team are, no doubt, domestic and international criminals. They and their supporters have decided that their ends justify their means, an arrogant blunder made many times in human history. Are we a nation of laws, not men?

If Clinton was impeachable for lying about having sex with "that woman," aren't the Bush violations just a bit more dangerous? Will they be held accountable? To paraphrase Senator McCain: "This is not about who the enemy is; it is about who we are."

WHAT IS A WAR CRIME?

Do we have a clear and consistent understanding of what a war crime is? We are certain that various foreign villains have committed war crimes. For example, Hitler, Stalin, Japanese troops in WW 2, and Saddam Hussein are all supposed to be war criminals beyond any doubt. On the other hand, I am sure many Americans don't think that war crimes are something American leaders could possibly authorize or commit. I suppose many Americans simply dismiss international law as irrelevant. Many believe, including President Bush, that we ought only be bound by our own laws and good intentions. Never mind that "the road to hell is paved with good intentions."

But connect the dots. Our law, the Constitution, says any treaties we ratify are part of the supreme law of our land. Among the treaties we have ratified, including the U.N. Charter and the Geneva Conventions, there is one we signed after World War 2 to prepare for prosecuting many Germans for war crimes. It was called Control Council Law No. 10, Punishment of Persons Guilty of War Crimes, Crimes Against Peace and Against Humanity. Our government ratified it with France, Britain, and the former Soviet Union.

That treaty defined "crimes against peace" as the:

> initiation of invasions of other countries and wars of aggression in violation of international laws and treaties, including but not limited to planning, preparation, initiation or waging a war of aggression, or a war in violation of international treaties or agreements.

We were happy to use this treaty to prosecute Germans for WW 2 crimes against peace.

Applying this treaty, we condemned the German invasions of Poland, Holland, France and the Soviet Union. Would an impartial jury decide that the Bush-Blair invasion of Iraq was a crime against peace?

This treaty's definition of "war crimes" included :

* offenses against persons or property
* murder or ill treatment of prisoners of war

* wanton destruction of cities, towns or villages not justified by military necessity

"Crimes against humanity" was defined to include:

* inhumane acts committed against any civilian population

What about the Rumsfeld shock-and-awe blitzkrieg attack on Iraq, the bombing and large scale devastation of many Iraqi cities, including Baghdad and Fallujah, the killings of more than 14,000 Iraqis? Would a jury judge that George W. Bush, Donald Rumsfeld, and others in the White House are war criminals for destroying Iraq in order to accomplish regime change? Could they be found guilty of crimes against humanity for devastating civilian population areas?

What about our treatment of "enemy combatants" and other detainees after 9-11? Would an impartial jury judge prisoners' indefinite detentions without being charged, without access to counsel, with the other abuses now being revealed, to be justified simply because the Bush regime felt this approach best for fighting terrorism? Would they agree that it was justified by "military necessity," or conclude it was simply an unnecessary extremist reaction to terrorism?

Remember that this law was not foisted on us by the United Nations. No, our leaders and

British leaders wanted this law in order to prosecute many of the losers in WW 2.

BUSH TEAM SANCTIONS TORTURE

There is now strong and extensive evidence, much of it coming from our own soldiers, that the Bush administration has been pursuing a policy of brutal interrogations, otherwise known as torture, of prisoners they think might have some possible information about terrorism in the world.

It has been happening systematically at Guantanamo Bay, in Afghanistan, in Iraq, and at secret detention centers in other nations. Sometimes, suspects are kidnapped and taken to be interrogated by officials in countries known to the world to use torture as their preferred interrogation techniques. This is called "rendition" by our secret police.

This violates the spirit if not the letter of the Geneva Conventions on treating prisoners of war humanely. Vice President Cheney has been especially persistent in openly pushing for the expanded use of tougher methods of getting information out of prisoners.

A court of law should hold these men accountable for the barbaric tactics they sanctioned in their crusade on terrorism. As Senator McCain has said, "This is not about them (the enemy). It is about us and the values we hold dear."

There are Americans who, no doubt, approve of this savage behavior, which almost never yields "actionable intelligence," useful information. Fortunately, there are also many Americans who deplore it, and we must recall that most Americans did not trust George W. Bush to be our President in 2000. So far, Mr. Bush and his cronies like Scooter Libby have shown poor and reckless judgment in carrying out their jobs.

It is hardly surprising that the Bush crew would goof up on the Harriet Miers nomination, but their overall unbalanced judgments are reaping us hell in our economy and hell in Iraq. Who will save us from the terrible consequences of Bush policies over the coming decades, of reaping what fanatics have sowed?

BUSH TEAM ARE EXTREMISTS

An extremist once proclaimed, "Extremism in the defense of liberty is no vice," and that Senator from Arizona remained a senator despite having lost his Presidential bid in a landslide to Lyndon Johnson. These days, the neocons and George W Bush don't bother to blather such extremist slogans; they just act them out. How times have changed?

A moderate, a liberal, once quietly said, "Extremism in anything is a vice," but such voices went unheard at the beginning of America's 21st Century. He said that "When extremists are in control, opposing them seems radical and fringe, but it is an honor to be fringe in such times."

Our nation is supposed to be all about citizens' rights to life, liberty, and property, and for each citizen to have the equal protection of the laws of any of our 50 states. We are a Republic, which means we are not to be ruled by kings or queens. Our government is supposed to promote the general welfare of the people, not mainly the wealthy and powerful.

"Republic" means for the public.

We now have a President who says he has the right to bend or disobey any of our laws if he judges it necessary for national security. You will not find even the hint of such executive prerogatives in our Constitution. Whether it concerns not keeping Congress informed, not allowing the courts to oversee spying on our citizenry, not honoring international law, being a warmonger, or detaining and brutalizing prisoners for years without charge or trial—this President behaves more like a king than the leader of a free nation.

Power tends to corrupt, and absolute power tends to corrupt absolutely. Our Founding Fathers were keenly aware of this. The abuse of power that I fear most, that I am most threatened by, is the power closest to me. That power is not Al Qaeda, Osama bin Laden, or the shadow world of global terrorism. That abusive power resides in the Bush White House and their fanatical supporters.

I am slightly consoled by recalling that most voters did not vote for Bush in 2000, and most Americans polled in recent months say they have no confidence in this President's ability to lead or to do the right thing. Truly, you cannot fool all of the people all of the time, or most Americans forever.

AMERICAN LEGION FASCISM

The American Legion (2.7 million members strong) has recently declared that there should be no more public protests against the war in Iraq. They say protesters should simply write letters to Congress or President Bush. At a recent convention in Hawaii, they voted to use whatever means are necessary to:

> ensure the united backing of the American people to support our troops and the global war on terrorism

We live in a flawed democracy, but it is one worth protecting and enhancing. The price of our freedom is eternal vigilance, for democracy can be frittered away and lost. It can easily be lost as citizens give more and more power to central government, usually out of fear of enemies abroad and at home.

This is how the fledgling German democracy of the 1930s was lost. Hitler's fascist party rose to power within the democratic process, and Hitler was elected to their parliament. As Germans suffered more and more from worldwide depression, and Hitler pledged to protect them from Middle Eastern terrorists (then it was Jews not Muslims), ordinary German citizens were ready for his strong man leadership when he seized absolute power. Ordinary Germans embraced Hitler's assertion that Germans were an exceptional people, meant to fulfill their destiny as world rulers.

People think that "fascism" is all about Hitler and Mussolini, but fascism goes way beyond those two historical examples. The Roman Empire was the inspiration for the very creation of this political philosophy. Fascism refers to the movement's emblem, the fasces, a bundle of rods bound around a projecting axehead that was carried before an ancient Roman magistrate by an attendant as a symbol of authority and power.

Fascism is all about authoritarian or dictatorial society in which opposition is censored or forcibly suppressed, a society guided by the belief that their people and culture are superior to other nations. Fascists believe that the lives of "their people" (because they are exceptional) are more worthy than those of inferior peoples.

Apparently, the Legionnaires simply dismiss our first amendment right to peaceably assemble and to petition our government to remedy grievances we have with government behavior. No doubt some of them are completely unaware of this Constitutional right we have as citizens of this republic.

During the old Cold War and under the Bush War on Terrorism, rightwing extremists feel free to spew their fascism in the name of patriotism. Shame on them, and shame on us if we allow them to destroy our democracy with their brutal and simpleton approach to the complex, real problems we face.

KING GEORGE AND ALBERTO

George W. Bush and his Attorney General, Alberto Gonzales, are now claiming the President has inherent authority which trumps all other considerations of law so long as the President acts in the name of national security. As long as the President believes that spying on U.S. citizens, or indefinite detentions without charge or trial, or "gloves off" interrogationssomehow protect the U.S.A.— Presidential authority reigns supreme.

Our Founding Fathers faced a dangerous world with hostile powers at home and abroad.

Empires—Spain and England—threatened U.S. security, to say nothing of the Indian nations at home. They nevertheless endorsed a nation with a bill of rights to protect them against their own government and a Constitution that put restraints on the power of any President. They had just rid themselves of King George; they didn't want another one at home masquerading as a President.

Consider the many security and war powers given by our Founding Fathers to the Congress. Congress has the exclusive authority:

* To declare war
* To define and punish piracies and felonies committed on the high seas, and offenses against the law of nations
* To make rules concerning captures made by our armed forces
* To raise and support armed forces (an army and navy in their era)
* To make rules for the government and regulation of the armed forces
* To provide for calling forth the militia to execute the laws of the union, suppress insurrections and repel invasions
* To provide for organizing, arming, and disciplining the militia
* To make all laws which shall be necessary and proper for carrying into execution the foregoing powers

They share authority with the President for the approval of treaties, ambassadors, and judges for our federal courts. Now notice what national security power is given exclusively to the President. The President shall be Commander in Chief of the armed forces of the United States, and of the Militia of the several States.

From this little phrase, "the Commander in Chief of the armed forces," Bush and Gonzales argue the President gains his inherent power to override all other law. Talk about pulling a big rabbit out of a tiny hat! You may be able to fool some of the people most of the time, especially the uninformed and fanatical true believers, but this is the royal viewpoint (fascism). If this President is allowed the authority of a King, our democracy is lost. We will go the way of ancient Rome as our Senate bows to our very own Caesar.

BUSH AND HITLER TOGETHER IN TIME

Recently, Time magazine chose President Bush as its man of the year. As I recalled how Time had also chosen Adolf Hitler as man of the year, back in 1938, it made me think about what I love and what I do not love about the U.S.A.

* I love the great beauty of our rivers, forests, lakes, mountains, valleys, and plains.
* I love the liberty guaranteed to us by our Constitution.

* I love our Constitution for guaranteeing the free expression of religious faith, no matter whether you are Christian, Jew, Muslim, Hindu, Buddhist, or whatever.
* I also love our Constitution for forbidding the government to establish any particular religion as the State Religion dictating to the rest of us how we must worship, pray, or live.
* I love the Constitution for giving us legal protections against our own government, against abusing "We the People." Thank goodness our founding fathers recognized that the power we need most fear is not a foreign power, but the corrupt or deluded righteousness of our own government officials. Officials cannot legally sneak and peak into our homes or personal effects (according to the 4th Amendment) fishing for information unless they first have a proper warrant describing the criminal evidence they imagine they will find.
* I love our Constitution for clearly giving almost all authority for overseeing our military and deciding when to go to war to the Congress (Article I, Sec. 8)—not the President (Article II, Sec. 2). Thus, we minimize the risk of the reckless and dictatorial use of our military might.

There is so much more about our country and Constitution that I love. I love my country, but I do not love many of our "leaders." I do not love ignorance, power lust, indifference, or cruelty.

* I do not love the fact that our government at all levels has been, and is, so prostituted to the interests of the very wealthy. This undermines true democracy.
* I do not love the fact that Time magazine editors are so awestruck by power and influence that they select people like Hitler and Bush to be their men of the year.

OUR LEADERS AS OUTLAWS

How nice it is that our leaders set such a fine example of obeying the laws of our nation!

Nixon systematically authorized illegal surveillance and burglaries, and he set up his own secret police, yet he was pardoned by his handpicked successor before being convicted of any crimes he was charged with. Reagan violated the Constitution and broke the law in his trading arms for hostages and in fighting a war in Nicaragua Congress specifically told him not to fight.

Bush and Cheney have violated our Constitution and international law so often it has become old news, unworthy of being harped on. They illegally authorize wiretaps and electronic eavesdropping in violation of the Foreign Intelligence Surveillance Act, they fight an illegal and horrid war in Iraq, and both claim they are immune from any oversight for any abuses they may have engaged in concerning national security.

Cheney even claims he is neither a member of the Executive nor the Legislative branch of our government. He seems to be the Fourth Pillar of our government, immune from any accountability.

Now Bush has commuted the sentence of Cheney's lap dog, Scooter Libby, so Libby will not have to spend any time in prison for obstruction of justice in the matter of finding out who improperly "outed" CIA operative, Valerie Plame, hence blowing her cover and threatening all her CIA covert contacts over her years of service. Cheney and Bush wanted this done to retaliate for her husband's efforts to tell the truth about the Bush-Cheney propaganda effort to prepare Congress and our public for invading Iraq.

Still, the GOP House of Representatives did manage to impeach Clinton for lying about having sex with his intern. Most of the world and most Americans found this a ludicrous waste of time.

Well, kids, just remember to obey the laws of our land and do what our leaders say you should. Do as they say, not as they do. What an example to set for our youth! We are all accountable for our actions—except people in high national office. If they say what they do is legal, it is. Another word for this is "Fascism."

A HOUSE DIVIDED

We (USA) Americans are sharply divided at present, and there is no use pretending otherwise. Appeals for patriotic unity at present are only slightly disguised appeals to join a certain point of view or ideology, to silence critics and those who disagree.

Since the Vietnam War disaster, our nation has been moving more and more toward a severe clash of worldviews and value systems. Many Americans safely avoid this by remaining as politically uninvolved and apathetic as possible. I would guess up to 40% of us fall into the uncommitted, undecided, usually non-voting category. We know that most U.S. adults choose not to vote and many choose not even to register to vote.

There is a passionate and activist minority of conservatives and right wingers (some on religious grounds and others on secular grounds), and there is a passionate and activist (smaller) minority of liberals and leftists. Conservatives tend to see Americans as righteous heroes and the rest of the world as in need of conversion to the American Way. Those foreigners who cooperate with us are civilized friends; those who do not are villains or savage enemies. Conservatives tend to be very suspicious of government unless it gives "their" money back to them or spends it on the military or national security agencies.

Liberals and leftists do not see our nation as automatically heroic and believe our government often acts like a villain. They think the civilized world extends far beyond our shores and that our leaders have no monopoly on wisdom or moral thinking. Liberals and leftists are suspicious of our own big government and big business. They think civilized reform begins at home and that we have a lot that needs reformed. They think the general welfare is just as important as individual opportunities to prosper in business.

There are many other deep divides between the left and right in this country. The two cultures are so different, and they share so little common ground, it is hard to see how they will learn to live together with peace and justice.

WE ARE DEEPLY DIVIDED

Slightly more than half of the voters voted for George W. Bush, and slightly less than half voted for Kerry. No doubt, this result will be treated as a Mandate from the voters, since so many Americans live in a LaLa land of fantasy and denial.

There will be appeals to get behind the President, to put behind us partisan bickering for the good of the country. The push for unity, even if only as a token, will be heard from many quarters. We in the opposition love our country, but despise most of Bush's policies.

The truth is that we were a deeply divided nation before Nov. 2, and we remain a deeply divided nation after Nov. 2. It is not a question of giving the President-elect a honeymoon period, a grace period, a benefit of the doubt until we see what he will do. George W. Bush has a public record, a disgraceful record.

He and his fanatical cabinet recklessly took us into an illegal war based on poor intelligence, a special problem for the President. He and his cronies are war criminals who are directly responsible for the unnecessary killings of thousands of Iraqi men, women, and children, to say nothing of thousands of American troops. His delusions and deceptions about this war, its connection to 9-11, and al Qaeda have bamboozled millions of Americans into support for the quagmire of Iraq.

Alas, you can't fool all of the people all of the time, but you can fool most Americans most of the time. They learned nothing from the deceptions and failures of the Vietnam war, and so we once again march down a dark road of ignorance, brutality and shame.

BEING RADICAL IN THE U.S.A.

Some citizens in our land, including some in government, think that extremism in the defense of liberty is no vice. This is wrong, of course, because extremism is always wrong, come hell or high water. By its very nature, extremist behavior is unbalanced, off track, and cannot hit the mark of moral righteousness.

We should distinguish between extremism in actions or policies and extremism in a person's ideas or goals. The great danger of extremism for society comes not from people whose ideas and goals are extremely different than mainstream thinking, but from people who feel their goals are so noble or pure that extreme measures can be used to accomplish their goals.

If some believe the U.S.A. is a corrupt and unworthy form of capitalism and if they are convinced it must be radically altered in order to bring about social justice and decency, they may still feel it is wrong to use violence to accomplish their goal. If some believe the U.S.A. is a shining city on a hill, bathed in God blessed liberty and justice for all, they may think brutal force at home and war abroad are necessary to protect and spread this gift.

Of course, these people have radically different visions of the U.S.A., but morally the significance lies in the means they are willing (or unwilling) to use in order to accomplish their ends. It is morally okay to have crazy goals so long as you do not use immoral methods to attain those goals. It is not morally okay to have a goal that you are willing to use immoral means to accomplish.

The true danger of extremism lies not in whether you think like most "normal" people think, but whether you think your ends justifies resorting to extremist methods. Government officials and mainstream citizens can be just as extremist as any radical, suicide bomber.

RULED BY EXTREMISTS

Since January of 2001, and especially since September 11 of 2001, we have been in the hands of extremists, both abroad and at home. Senator Barry Goldwater once said that extremism in the defense of liberty is no vice, but speaking plainly, extremism is always a vice, no matter how we rationalize it.

There were many sane and sober ways of our responding to the horrors of 9-11.

Our President did not have to declare a perpetual war against global terrorism, a war which could not be won and would be fought against nations rather than the terrorists who move within their borders. No method of battling terrorism guarantees that no more acts of terror will occur, so no method can be justified as an absolute way of preventing future terrorism. That no such acts have occurred within the US in two years hardly shows that the Bush tactics will keep us safe.

Speaking loudly and wielding a big stick may work in some street fights, but it is a terribly poor strategy for dealing with international issues like terrorism. Other nations resent being coerced and bullied to follow the wishes of one or two nations' leaders. They want to fight terrorism, but not in Bush's way, which they regard as extremist and misguided. So we lose their goodwill and isolate ourselves, making it just that much harder to battle terrorism.

A moderate and sane approach to fighting terrorism would look like the following. First, understand the reasons why people at home and abroad come to hate your government and its policies. Answering in cartoon stereotypes like "they hate our freedom" and simply are "evildoers" show that you have not tried to understand these reasons. Second, enlist the help of other governments, their police and armed forces to locate and arrest suspected terrorists so they can be put on trial for the crimes committed. Third, you target very specifically (economically and militarily) terrorists, but never wage war against entire nations in order to strike at a few terrorists. Fourth, you obey international law in your struggle against terrorism, rejecting the extremist idea that because terrorists disobey international law, so you too are entitled to be an outlaw.

A cliché we hear over and over again is that 9-11 changed everything. No it didn't. Not everyone who was intelligent or balanced prior to 9-11 flipped out and became an idiot as a result of 9-11. Furthermore, for most of the world, everyday life prior to 9-11 was filled with fear, hunger and violence, and this remained their fate after 9-11.

Extremists think that everything changed after 9-11, but that does not in any way justify their extremist way of thinking or acting. Who will protect us against the right wing extremism that now grips our nation and threatens to destroy our future?

RIGHT WING HYSTERIA

Yesterday I was listening to Rush Limbaugh rant and rave about the terrorist attacks in London. He said he was filled with anger about many things, then went on to give his sermon about the terrible events.

He said the attacks had nothing to do with Iraq, and they were not attacks on London or England. Instead, he said they were attacks on our Western values and culture. He scolded liberals and leftists for not realizing that we must either surrender to terrorism or defeat it. He insisted we cannot reason or negotiate with these kinds of people because they are not rational or moral.

How did Rush discover this about terrorists? Does he think they are crazy because they use lethal violence against civilians to accomplish their goals? But our government and most governments are also willing to kill civilians to accomplish our ends. They call it collateral damage. Is it because they are willing to sacrifice their lives through suicide attacks to further their cause? But being willing to die for country or cause is honored in wartime.

Of course, the attacks in London were against England for Blair's support of the war in Iraq. Of course, they were in retaliation for England's role in throwing Afghanistan and Iraq into deeper chaos and misery than they had known under the Taliban or Saddam. The London bombings were savage and immoral. The attackers probably felt likewise about our bombings of Iraq and Afghanistan, where many thousands of civilians have suffered and died as "collateral damage." War is hell.

As for the idea we must surrender to terrorism or defeat it, no one favors surrender. Neither does anyone know what "defeating" terrorism means, any more than we know what defeating murder, drugs, crime, or sin means. Does this mean giving up terror as a tool in Shock-and-Awe bombing or as a tool in interrogating "enemy combatants?"

How to cope with terrorism is the real issue before us, not the simpleton choices people like Limbaugh and Bush try to force on us. We must begin by understanding the enemy (which is different from forgiveness or offering therapy, Mr. Rove) and by understanding our government's part in creating the enemy. The second step is to join most of the civilized world in treating terrorism as an international crime to be fought by police, prosecutors, judges, juries, and prisons.

Waging war against "terrorism" is a blunt and indiscriminate response which creates more enemies than it destroys. If we bury our heads in the sand of cartoon stereotypes, seeing ourselves as Righteous Heroes fighting an army of Darth Vaders, we will surely fail, and the world will be made worse as we pave the road to hell with our ill-informed good intentions.

BUSH'S PERPETUAL WAR

President Bush and his partisan supporters say his war against terrorism is succeeding, and we are safer today as a result. Is this true, and how do we know it?

Over the Christmas holiday, the Bush administration put our nation on the highest state of alert since 9/11. Does this mean we are safer?

At some point, sober-minded people will be forced to ask themselves, "How can we tell if the Bush approach is working?"

Only the most hard core of right wing extremists will be content to fight a never-ending war against evildoers worldwide, especially as our soldiers continue to die and U.S. prestige continues to plunge.

Most people are not prepared to accept the 21st-century version of a crusade against witches, unbelievers, Communists — the shadowy evildoers of paranoid fantasies.

Will the Bush approach be working if terrorist attacks against Western troops and targets continue in many nations in the world, in spite of the aggressive use of our armed forces worldwide? Will it be working if occasionally we capture the alleged leader of enemy forces, say Saddam or Osama? Will it be working if our nation continues to go into deeper debt and cut back on domestic programs to pay for the war on terrorism? Will it be working if world opinion continues to go against the U.S. method of fighting terrorism?

Look to the way Israel has chosen to fight Palestinian commandos (or terrorists) for the past half century. Is Israel safer? Have Israelis had many secure nights' sleep in over 50 years? No. If we follow the government of Israel's path, I feel we will have perpetual war with no clue about how to end the carnage.

ANOTHER VIETNAM

What a war! What a mess! Our troops are there, we are told, to liberate and to bring democracy. They are there to support an elected government against a vicious minority which hates democracy and human rights.

It is a very difficult war because the people there are from a culture so different from our American culture. Their religion is different, and we don't even speak their language. Our troops cannot tell enemy from foe in this kind of guerilla warfare, and sometimes we shoot first and ask questions later. There have been atrocities committed by some soldiers, but our military has brought them to trial and found some guilty as charged.

Nearly half of Americans oppose the war, but the public is told we must be patient, stay the course, and support the troops. Our government says that we can expect many years of fighting before the enemy is finally defeated. Still, government officials say they see signs the enemy has been weakened, signs we are making progress.

Many nations oppose our effort, and the United Nations refuses to lend us their support. To make matters worse, the enemy there is being supplied and supported by allies in neighboring nations. Until those borders can be secured, our enemy will continue to receive supplies and more people to fight against us.

Is this the above about Iraq or Vietnam? For those of you old enough to remember Vietnam, what do you think? What do you Vietnam veterans say? Forget the WMD issue. We all now know there were none, and the Bushies say it doesn't matter. As Pilate said, "What is truth?"

Aren't we repeating an historic mistake of tragic proportions? Did our two decades of war in Vietnam (beginning in 1955 under President Eisenhower) liberate their people for democracy, or did they become Communist?

PANEL TO INVESTIGATE BUSH TEAM INTELLIGENCE

President Bush has now realized that there needs to be some sort of independent inquiry into the poor intelligence surrounding claims that Iraq had WMDs and posed a clear and present dangerto this nation and other nations. Mr. Bush and his National Security Council face a credibility problem. Gadzooks, his approval rating is now below 50%.

Whatever some Bush supporters may now say was a good reason for our nation to invade Saddam's Iraq, prior to going to war the Bush regime emphasized Iraq's having WMDs, including possible nuclear weapons, as the reason our Congress, our public, and the international community should support war against Iraq. The point hammered home time and time again, including by Secretary Powell at the United Nations, was that we could not afford to give UN inspectors more time to search for Iraqi alleged WMDs. The time had come to enforce UN resolutions by invading Iraq. We dare not risk a mushroom cloud over a city in the U.S.

Now the facts seem directly contrary to the Bush-Blair claims about the WMDs possessed by Iraq. They apparently had zero weapons of mass destruction. The panel Mr. Bush will appoint is to investigate the reasons for the poor intelligence given to Mr. Bush.

One issue is: was the information given President Bush really that poor, or did the President and his advisors selectively pay heed only to information that supported their desire for regime change in Iraq? Were questions asked about the nature of human sources of intelligence? Did they seek independent sources to corroborate claims made?

In other words, were they given poor intelligence, or did the Bush team lack enough intelligence to honestly assess the information given them?

Another issue is: how independent and credible will Mr. Bush's inquiry commission be? To have maximum credibility, the commission members should not be selected by President Bush. Otherwise, selections can be handpicked to more or less guarantee no very embarrassing outcome. Furthermore, the commission should not be made up of present or former leaders in the two major parties since both parties showed great support for Bush's rush to war in Iraq. The commission should be composed of Independents, or at least not by the same old bipartisan warriors from both sides of the aisle.

The Warren Commission is an excellent example of how not to conduct an independent inquiry. From the outset, they declared their intention to assure the American public that one man and one man only shot President Kennedy. In an arena where it makes sense to consider possible conspiracies (ask Julius Caesar), the Warren Commission decided it was not a live option. An inquiry with integrity must allow the facts to determine whether there has been dirty play in politics, not allow political hacks to assure us that all is well.

DON'T STAY THE COURSE!

Recently, Mr. Fish wrote a letter about the need for people to be patient concerning the changes taking place in Iraq. Patience is indeed a virtue, but the war in Iraq was spawned by impatience and reckless abandon.

If patience is good, then why was the Bush regime not patient with the United Nations and their arms inspectors? Our government has shown incredible patience with Israel, although Israel has been, by far, the most frequent violator of UN Security Council resolutions.

As virtually all informed people realized, it was unlikely that Saddam still had the weapons of mass destruction our government had helped him acquire to fight against Iran. It was also ludicrous to suggest he posed a grave threat, having been crushed in the first Gulf War, to the Middle East or the United States.

If Bush simply had been patient and allowed the inspectors to complete their work, they would have discovered what we all now know. There were no WMDs to be found there. It does no good to urge everyone to be patient with a war policy which was founded on impatience.

Here is another sticking point. Basic morality we teach our kids says: the goodness of our goal does not mean that we can use immoral means to accomplish our goal. As patience is a virtue, so too the end does not justify the means. Almost everyone around the world would agree that getting a real democracy for Iraq is a wonderful goal. How you get there makes all the difference.

You cannot wage illegal, aggressive war to bring about a democracy in another land. The citizens of that country must choose to wage that revolution for overthrowing the abusive government. You cannot tell a people: Choose democracy, or we will kill you and destroy much of your nation. Sanctions against Saddam (between the Gulf wars) cost at least 500,000

Iraqi kids their lives, and the current war and occupation has killed as many as 100,000 Iraqis.

We fought our own revolution to kick out the British. This is not what happened in Iraq. The war was sold on reckless falsehoods about WMDs and mushroom clouds over our cities, and Iraq was shocked and awed into rubble in order to get rid of Saddam. With friends like us, I am sure many Iraqis ask, "Who needs enemies?"

O'NEILL REVEALS BUSH'S DECEIT IN PUSHING FOR WAR

Finally, a Bush administration insider has blown the lid off the lies about the Iraq war. Paul O'Neill was Bush's treasury secretary for two years, removed from his post because he disagreed with the Bush tax cut plan.

O'Neill says the Bush team began planning for regime change, and war if necessary, in Iraq almost as soon as they took office in 2001, long before 9/11. They simply had to wait to find the right story to tell the American people to justify their war plans.

For those who follow international news closely, it was clear that, contrary to Bush-Blair claims to the contrary, there was almost no chance Saddam still possessed weapons of mass destruction or that he posed a threat to us or even his Middle Eastern neighbors. Saddam's army and air force had been devastated by the first Gulf War, over a decade of severe sanctions, and controlled only about a third of Iraq, the north and the south having been carved into no-fly zones patrolled by U.S.-led air power.

For right-wing supporters of the Bush regime, such facts and O'Neill's blowing their cover won't make any difference. Their extremist ideology is just fine with our nation controlling world politics as if it were a grand chessboard, using great violence if necessary. In their cartoon worldview, we must be a bully or be bullied. For America's silent majority, those who pay only scattered attention to international affairs, the sad truth is that they have been manipulated into supporting war. You can't fool all of the people all of the time, but you can fool most of the people most of the time.

UNITED WE STAND FOR PEACE

As most of the world knew before the war began and as a majority of Americans now understand, it was an awful mistake to invade Iraq and there is no likely way to win the Bush-Blair war. Our troops have done their duty. They and their families can be proud of the troops beating Saddam's army and deposing the former dictator.

How can some still believe more G.I.s must die in order to justify the death of the 2000 plus who have already died in this Bush-Blair folly? Fact: Iraq posed no military threat to its neighbors or the world after being badly beaten in the first Iraq war. Fact: No evidence from any credible source exists that Saddam still had WMDs in 2003, that Iraq was a training ground for terrorism, or that Iraq was in any way connected to 9-11. Fact: As a direct result of the Bush-Blair invasion of Iraq, Iraq now is an intense training ground for Al Qaeda and attacks on the U.S.

Before being invaded, Iraq was ruled by a tyrant, but they had a stable society with high employment. After the invasion, Iraqi society was in chaos with very low employment. There may well be a civil war and blood bath after we leave Iraq. By the way, there is now a blood bath ongoing in Iraq. We too have had our own civil war, and we recovered from it.

It is time for Bush-Blair to get out of Iraq and leave Iraq to the Iraqis. If Bush is sincere in his denial of our imperial designs, he can pledge not to keep military bases on Iraqi soil. If not, more Bush deception will be exposed.

We need as Americans (like Rep. Murtha) to unite behind a new stand for peace. Can we at last pledge "For peace, united we stand?"

FIGHT OVER THERE, NOT OVER HERE

George W. Bush, his regime, and many of his supporters like to say with passion that we have to wage war in Iraq and Afghanistan so that we don't have to fight the terrorists here in our homeland. This is a tired, old slogan: "Over there, not over here."

Like many emotional slogans, this one has no merit when thought out. To begin with, rightwing internet bloggers aside, Iraq had no connection with the plan to attack us on 9-11. This was confirmed by the 9-11 Commission report. Attacking Iraq because of 9-11 would have been like attacking Romania for the Japanese attack on Pearl Harbor.

The kind of enemy attack from terrorism we have to fear is the kind that happened on 9-11. Whether they try to attack us with 747s as missiles, place bombs on incoming sea vessels, or try some other kind of domestic sabatoge—such terrorism is handled by the Coast Guard and tightened security measures here in the U.S. Also, using diplomacy and putting terrorists on trial works. Recently, two people received death sentences in a foreign court for their conviction in attacking our U.S.S. Cole.

Osama and Al Qaeda, and any other foreign groups that hate our government's behavior overseas, will not launch conventional war against us because they are no match for our conventional armed forces. Aside from protecting our two ocean borders, we have only to more carefully guard our Canadian and Mexican borders.

The only result of waging preemptive, first strike wars against other nations to pursue the "war on terrorism" is to create more hatred against our government and the U.S.A. We are perceived as arrogant occupiers willing to sacrifice tens of thousands of other nations' civilians as the collateral damage price of getting a few evildoers. The Bush crusade is only breeding new armies of terrorists in the Middle East and the Afghanistan-Pakistan region.

The fanatical, simpleton war policy of the Bush regime must be stopped before the whole world is burning in the chaos paved with the intentions of hate-filled zealots.

CIVIL WARS AND BLOOD BATHS

Many who support the Bush-Blair invasion and occupation of Iraq say we cannot just leave Iraq because if we do, there will be a civil war and blood bath. The likelihood of the invasion producing this kind of chaos, and possible civil war, in Iraq was predicted by our own C.I.A. in a National Defense Estimate. This prediction was dismissed by President Bush, saying "they are just guessing." Does the record show that President Bush has good judgment?

Our nation has some experience of civil war and blood bath from our own history. When the South decided their irreconcilable differences with the North could only be settled by the South leaving the Union, both sides chose war, our bloodiest war, a war which killed over 600,000 Americans. It was a time of suffering and chaos.

Did our civil war destroy us? No, we arose from the war stronger than we had been before. Although the South suffered from the loss, it did arise again, and now is one of the most influential regions in our nation. Many of our recent Presidents have come from the South.

Imagine if two great foreign powers, say England and France, had decided to invade and occupy our nation in order to prevent such a civil war and blood bath, and also to bring justice to those who sponsored slavery. Of course, there was no dictator to remove, but the treatment of the slaves was a massive crime against humanity.

You know there would have been great U.S. resistance, and a strong insurgency, to kick the meddling foreigners out of our country. Few Americans would have trusted the English or French motives for the military intervention. Even if few took up arms against the foreigners, most Americans would have sympathized with ending the foreign occupation.

Most of us would have believed the occupiers were here for our natural resources and political power. Not knowing who the insurgents were because we didn't wear uniforms and used sneak attacks on their soldiers, the French and British probably would have killed lots of civilians and detained many more for tough interrogation.

Would they have succeeded in imposing a more humane order on our country? Will Bush and Blair succeed in Iraq?

WHITE HOUSE LACKING ETHICS

There is a pattern of reckless disregard for the truth in this White House.

We saw it with reference to wild and sometimes forged claims about Iraq seeking uranium from Africa, having weapons of mass destruction (Rumsfeld said we knew where they are) and being a grave threat to world security. We saw it when now discredited CIA Director Tenet said that the information we had proving the current existence of Saddam's WMDs was a "slam dunk."

Now, we learn that conservative pundit Armstrong Williams was paid $240,000 with taxpayer money by the Bush White House to push Bush's "No Child Left Behind" program. This is paying for propaganda. Maybe, Bush will award Williams with a medal of freedom like he awarded George Tenet for telling Congress the story Bush wanted them to hear.

This cabal in the White House are fanatics who believe their goals justify their means. They systematically ignore and distort the truth, even paying their 30 pieces of silver to hire Armstrong

Williams to perpetuate their propaganda. By the way, who is profiting from the Iraqi oil our soldiers are guarding? Big oil companies or the Iraqi people? Research it. Follow the money trail if you want truth about Iraq.

Their distortions and propaganda have killed thousands upon thousands in a criminal war in Iraq. Meanwhile, these distortions have pushed our nation into record debt, which our kids and grandkids will have to pay for while being told that needed domestic programs have to be cut or eliminated.

"Moral values" in this White House? Not truth, that is for sure. Not protecting the thousands of civilian lives lost as collateral damage in the War on Terrorism. Protecting human life takes a lot more than being anti-abortion and bashing gay marriage. This extremist regime in the White House is so blinded by their cartoon ideology and their upper class warfare against the rest of us that they are unable to tell truth from falsehood.

They have many working class guys convinced that silver-spoon-fed George W is just an ordinary guy like the rest of them. Our rulers like cute slogans for naming their wars and battle plans. I have one for Bush and Karl Rove's shameful approach to governing: Operation Urgent Deception.

STAY THE COURSE, SUPPORT DELUSION

1862 Americans (92 from Pennsylvania) have been killed so far in this war which began in March 2003. This compares with 1864 Americans killed in the Vietnam War in the early years: 1961-1965.

It is hard to exaggerate how many mistaken judgments President Bush and his team have made about Iraq. To mention a few, there were the weapons of mass destruction, the ties to Al Qaeda, Iraq posing a grave threat to national security, and our troops being greeted as liberators. Now they want us to be patient with the process of drafting and approving a Constitution for the new Iraq while reminding us that it took 12 years to approve our own Constitution after we declared our independence from King George in 1776.

Guess what, we didn't have our independence or Constitution imposed on us by an invading power whose leaders insisted we become democratic. We waged an insurgency (the Brits called our Sons of Liberty "The Sons of Violence") against an imperial power, we won, and we formulated our own Constitutional process and destiny. Maybe you've noticed that often people resent "outside agitators."

The Iraqi National Assembly, unable to agree on the draft of a new Constitution and operating under their transitional law, has broken the law by extending their deadline for completing a draft Constitution. The Law of Administration for The State of Iraq For The Transitional Period states that any such extension must be made by August 1, 2005— not the wee hours of August 15. That law also states that if the August 15 deadline is not met, the National Assembly is dissolved and the process begins again from scratch. Can Iraqis be united behind leaders who break their own basic laws?

Most members of Congress (Democrat and Republican) and President Bush will not be bothered much by this new setback. Our national leaders in both parties are quite accustomed to violating our Constitution and international law whenever it suits them. Both Democrats and Republicans in Congress have long ago abandoned their own Constitutional authority in order to treat our Presidents more like Kings than chief executive officers.

I guess this tells us what kind of democracy our leaders and their rightwing supporters want for Iraq. Like our own country, they want people in power who will obey the laws when it suits them and break them when it suits them. In this way, they support "United We Stand." It is also the kind of habitual abuse of power which led Jefferson to write that under some circumstances the people have the right and the duty to alter or abolish their government.

STANDING DOWN IN IRAQ

What is the real Bush strategy for removing our troops from Iraq? We hear cute slogans like "When the Iraqis stand up, we will stand down," but what is the substantive plan?

We were told for nearly 20 years in the Vietnam War that when the South Vietnamese Army were able to stand on its own, we could leave Vietnam. Guess what? They never could stand up, so we had to cut and run. This cut and run strategy was the creation of GOP President Nixon, which he called (in the typical Orwellan spin that our government loves) "peace with honor."

The South Vietnamese government could not stand on its own because the people of Vietnam did not see their government as legitimate or honorable. They saw it as the ongoing creation of a foreign occupying power. Guess who that foreign power was from 1955-1974? They saw their rulers as corrupt puppets of the United States.

If Bush and his neoconservative backers really plan to leave Iraq and not to be an imperial power in the Middle East, why are large military bases being built there? President Bush should swear that these bases will not be placed there for 50 or 60 years like our military in South Korea. By the way, have the South Koreans gained the ability stand up? If so, why are our troops and tactical nuclear weapons still deployed in and near South Korea?

It would be nice to be able, in good conscience, to give Bush the benefit of the doubt about his intentions in Iraq, but so far, his record of failed intelligence and predictions does not merit such trust. When the Bush true believers say we should trust in the Bush policy toward Iraq or terrorism, it reminds me of a Clinton true believer saying that Clinton did not have "sex with that woman." One day, I am sure these newspeak loyalists will explain the Bush noble policy to me in terms that are as clear as the many definitions of `is'.

GLOBAL WARMING DISMISSED

The first seven months of this year are the hottest ever recorded in the United States. Most of the hottest years on record worldwide have occurred within the past 20 years. NASA and other scientists have documented the rapid melting of the Arctic ice mass and the Antarctic ice mass.

The overwhelming consensus among climatologists and oceanographers is that global warming has been a growing menace, caused substantially by the human release of carbon emissions into the atmosphere. Precisely how bad this will be for us is still uncertain, but the extreme weather will cause immense suffering for people all over our planet.

Meanwhile, neoconservatives, George Bush, and deep thinkers like Rush Limbaugh continue to pooh pooh the whole issue. Their response has been as follows. "It ain't happening, maybe it is but we humans didn't cause it, and it is a liberal conspiracy to undermine America and the free enterprise system." They even found a few scientists to say they thought global warming wasn't happening.

To the neocons, it seems the big issues are banning gay marriage, abortion, and flag burning. Also, a top priority is unquestioned support for whatever Bush does in the name of national security and more tax "relief" for our poor wealthy Americans.

Aside from being mean-spirited, a bit paranoid, and terribly ignorant of science, I guess the view of extreme conservatives is that they would rather go to hell than believe liberals are right about anything. Guess what, I think they are going to get their wish. I only wish they weren't dragging the rest of us with them as they fiddle while the Earth burns.

BORN IN THE USA

I was born in the USA in the Wild, Wild West of Wyoming. This country is my home, the home of my parents, my wife, my son, and my friends. I love our ideals of liberty and justice for all. Having to live away from home would be a sad and lonely fate.

Before I could think for myself, I learned to deeply admire our Revolutionary War and Honest Abe's freeing of the slaves. Later, this got mixed in with other idols like Davy Crocket, Mickey Mantle, Arnold Palmer, and rock music.

Now our nation is in the midst of a Bush led crusade to bring freedom and democracy to the rest of the world. Freedom and democracy are great, especially when they are chosen rather than forced on you through the terrorism of war.

I wonder if we all hear the same thing when we hear "freedom" or "democracy." Maybe some hear "freedom to pursue the love of money, oil, power, or convenience" while others hear "free and fair elections" or "freedom from torture or secret police abuse." So far, in Operation Enduring Freedom, many Iraqis have been liberated from life by the U.S. led coalition.

I wonder about the commitment we have to liberty and justice in our own country. Our founding fathers didn't think voting rights should extend to women or people without property. They owned slaves, and treated the Indians with treachery and a trail of broken promises. Official segregation in the South didn't begin to end until the mid 1950s. Thousands of Japanese Americans were rounded up and put in concentration camps during WW 2, and over one thousand people, especially

Arab and Muslim, have been rounded up and detained indefinitely here in the U.S. since 9-11.

We have only two major political parties, and they are dominated by big money and extremist ideology. No wonder then that, for the last half century, most of our citizens of voting age choose not to vote for any candidate or party.

Liberty: with this record of "promoting" democracy at home, perhaps people around the world can be forgiven if they are skeptical when told they must embrace democracy or risk war with the United States. Justice: for Christians, shouldn't it be important to note what Jesus said about those who would mete out death for breaking the law? "Let he who is without sin cast the first stone."

LOVE OF COUNTRY

I love what the flag means to me. There is the unity amidst diversity signified by the 50 stars, one for each State of our United States. I love the red and white stripes for reminding me of the original thirteen colonies and the blood spent to break away from King George and to gain our nation's independence.

I love the flag for reminding me that ours is a nation pledged to respect laws and respect for basic human rights rather than the will of an elite few. I love the fact that our Declaration of Independence said if our government becomes abusive of we the people over a long period of time, we have the right and the duty to rise up against our government and replace it with any sort of government we choose.

I love the fact that our Constitution contains the "Bill of Rights" which pledges us protection against the abuse of power by our own government. I love the fact that our Founding Fathers gave most of the power over our military, including war-declaring power, to our Congress not the President. (I am saddened that few citizens are aware of this and that our Congress chooses not to assert their Constitutional authority over Presidents.)

I love our immense freedom (and am saddened to see it under such attack these days in the name of fighting terrorism). I love baseball, football, and basketball, hamburgers, hot dogs, apple pie, rock music, Hendrix' national anthem, and the chance every few years to vote the rascals out of office. I love the land of my birth, and I am sad that so many of us choose to be poorly informed, avoid participating in politics, and allow elites to run our lives.

America, the land of shining ideals, is worth saving, but time is running out.

SENATE'S TRADITIONAL FILIBUSTER REMAINS CONSTITUTIONAL

The battle over President Bush's radical nominees to our federal courts and other agencies continues. Some conservatives are now arguing that the Democrat filibuster in the Senate to prevent a vote on these nominees is actually unconstitutional.

They charge that a president is entitled to have his nominees voted on and approved or disapproved by a majority vote. The filibuster, they argue, violates this rule by allowing a minority to block a vote on a nominee so long as the majority cannot get at least a two thirds vote to end the filibuster.

They are not telling us the truth. Here is what the Constitution says on this issue:

> He shall have Power... and by and with the Advice and Consent of the Senate, shall appoint Ambassadors, other public Ministers and Consuls, Judges of the Supreme Court, and all other Officers of the United States" (Article 11, Section. 2).

It neither endorses nor prohibits the Senate from using a two thirds vote, a majority vote, or a Ouija board as their way of giving their advice and consent. Which rule they use is left up to the Senate to decide.

I am not in favor of the filibuster as a matter of principle, but the rules of the Congress must be applied evenhandedly and fairly. If the filibuster is a bad idea, it should be not allowed in any cases by either side of the political aisle.

It has been used pervasively by both Democrats and Republicans to block the other side when the minority wanted to block the majority on a variety of issues, often when they feared a nominee would be too left-wing or right-wing in their ideology.

It was unconstitutional for the president and the Senate to invade Iraq because it violated the United Nations Charter and Geneva Conventions, which are now part of the supreme law of our land due to Article VI, Clause 2, which says:

> This Constitution, and the Laws of the United States which shall be made in Pursuance thereof, and all Treaties made, or which shall be made, under the Authority of the United States, shall be the supreme Law of the Land.

It is not unconstitutional for the Senate to use a Ouija board, the toss of a coin or a two thirds rule when approving or disapproving appointees to our courts or other federal posts.

PAYING OUR DUES

Many people take for granted that tax cuts and tax relief are wonderful things, things conservatives favor while liberals oppose. After all, so the reasoning goes, it is our money, and we are better off with it than those damnable government bureaucrats.

Phrases like `tax relief' are wonderful spin words, suggesting the need for relief from tax `burdens', conjuring up innocent victims who need to be saved by those good-Samaritan conservatives. Yet this is nothing but distortion, propaganda and narcissism.

We can always debate spending levels for particular programs run with public funds, but the need for taxes—our dues—is bottom line. To chant about the evils of taxes, tax burdens, and the need for tax relief is often just a cover in code words for thoughtless and selfish thinking. Naturally, the wealthy are not as harmed by the loss of public revenues since they can afford to pay for services out of their own pockets. The quick fixes of dues reductions—tax cuts—are most appreciated by the wealthy and those who serve them.

When you live in civilized society, you owe dues as a citizen. Most of us need to pool our 'dues', i.e. tax revenues, to pay for services we need or want. No one is entitled to a free ride, to be a parasite on the rest of us. Our dues pay for police, fire departments, highway maintenance, snow removal, safety inspectors for food and workplace dangers, environmental clean up, Medicare, Social Security, armed forces for defense, and many more social services.

If a person doesn't want to pay his or her dues, that's all right, but they can't stay here to freeload. Love it or leave it!

POLITICAL SIGNS

Recently, Mr. Wood wrote a letter complaining about the unattractive clutter of political signs around voting time. He claimed the signs are ineffective for the most part, and those who were influenced by them should have their voting "privilege" rescinded.

I agree with him that the signs are unattractive and a clutter nuisance, but real democracy is messy and a nuisance. Life is much more efficient and orderly in a fascist state like Saudi Arabia or WW 2 Germany and Italy.

I am sure that many of us are not influenced in any positive way by candidates' political signs, but I am also sure some of us are. In elections where few people vote (the rule in our country), a few votes can make all the difference. The point is to gain name recognition so that voters will be more likely to flip the lever for you on Election Day. In our society the more successful candidates do this by spending lots of money on radio and TV ads. Most candidates for local office, especially fairly minor offices, cannot afford "big bucks" campaigns, so they settle for what they can afford.

The game of being elected in our country is Name Recognition and Money. That's how we play it. Don't blame the little guys and gals for their efforts to play the game. Anyhow, in a democracy, voting is not a privilege, but our right as citizens.

NEEDED ELECTION REFORM

Most Americans know we need serious election reform, and not simply to avoid hanging chads or corrupt Florida politics. We need to rejuvenate our election system to bring many more citizens to the polls and to minimize the excessive influence of money. We don't want to be known as the best democracy money can buy.

We need to have spending limits and public financing of our elections, beginning at the national level for Congress and the President. A spending cap will be set to guarantee that, whether through public or private funding, no candidate or party can buy an election. Money will go to candidates based on the percentage of votes their party won in the prior election, an equal portion going to all those who garnered a minimum percentage of votes in the prior election, say 30 %. These candidates would be considered major party candidates. Lesser amounts would go to those candidates whose party received lower percentages of votes in the last election. Beneath a certain threshold, say

5%, the candidate would receive no public funding. Candidates not eligible for public funding could still run for office, but they could spend no more than the amount permitted major party candidates. These cost controls would make our elections far cleaner and more democratic.

No campaign ads other than those paid for by each candidate's campaign would be allowed. Independent campaign ad support from corporations, labor unions, wealthy individuals, environmental groups, and other lobbying interests would be forbidden. This limits freedom of expression, but is a needed trade off to prevent elections from being sold to the highest bidders.

There should be a short campaign season, say three months prior to the November elections. All political ads (TV, radio, signs, posters, etc.) for candidates running for the House, Senate, or President would have to occur during those three months. This would eliminate the rationale for raising huge campaign chests, and it would allow voters to concentrate on the election. Who needs to be bored or numbed by several years of campaigning? All national news networks would be obliged (to retain their FCC license) to give free coverage to any debates between candidates during the three months political campaign.

Election day should be a holiday, or the election should be a weekend in November (allowing people two days to vote), thereby making it extremely convenient for any registered voter to cast their ballot. If we really want registered voters to vote, we should have a system that encourages voting.

Finally, we should amend our Constitution to eliminate the "electoral college" in choosing Presidents. "One person, one vote" should be our commitment to democracy. There is no reason why certain regions should carry more weight than others. There is no more wisdom in people simply because they are from the West, South, East, or North. Florida may be a great place for retirement, sunshine and the Cuban mafia, but it should not have the final say in who becomes President. The current system has long undermined our claim to be a champion of democracy.

DYSFUNCTIONAL DEMOCRACY

How about a reality check on the pulse of our "democracy?" According to figures compiled by the Federal Election Commission, we can look at trends of voter apathy or alienation over the past several decades.

In 1976 when Jimmy Carter ran against Gerald Ford, 60 million voters-of-age-to-vote (a larger group than registered voters) chose not to vote. In 1980 when Ronald Reagan ran against Jimmy

Carter, 77 million voters-of-age-to-vote chose not to vote. In 1992 when Bill Clinton ran against Ross Perot and George H.W. Bush, 72 million voters-of-age-to-vote chose not to vote. In 2000 when George W. Bush ran against Ralph Nader and Al Gore, 100 million voters-of-age-to-vote chose not to vote.

When this many citizens, election after election, choose not to vote, can we assume that our government represents "We, the people" as the preamble to our Constitution says? Don't we need to admit that our Presidents are elected by a minority of voting age citizens?

Can we call ourselves The Model for democracy around the world? Can we dismiss all or most of these people as lazy and apathetic? Could it be that tens of millions of Americans do not vote because they believe neither the Democrats nor the Republicans represent their values, dreams and hopes?

The truth is that our nation is and has been from its inception more of an oligarchy, rule by the wealthy few, than a nation in which there is rule by and for the people. A long struggle ensued to give African-Americans and women the right to vote, and much later came the right to vote for young people who could be sent to war. But from the beginning, a wealthy elite has found many ways to ensure that their voices will count more than the ballot box.

The color of political success in our nation is the green color of loads of money to underwrite election campaigns and allegiance to the "bottom line" of corporate agendas. If any political party manages to attract the tens of millions of citizens who normally choose not to vote, there could well be a seismic shock in U.S. politics.

LIVING IN LA-LA LAND

My country has evolved into a La-La land of Orwellian doublespeak. We say we are a nation of laws, not men. Everyone is supposed to be bound by our laws, from the President to the plumber, but our presidents are allowed to violate their oath of office and Constitution with barely a murmur from Congress or anyone else.

In the name of national security, Presidents Johnson, Reagan, and George W. Bush have committed serious breaches of their oath of office by violating our Constitution and lying to Congress and the public about what they were doing. Presidents are not held accountable for impeachable offenses unless the indiscretion involves adultery or oral sex. People say doing so would cause the nation too much trauma.

Since both Democratic and Republican presidents have committed high crimes and misdemeanors, neither party is willing to make this an issue. We are ruled by bipartisan cowardice and corruption. Their sins are the love of money and power.

Anyhow, what do you do if the laws of your land are authored by a minority of wealthy people who are obligated mainly to people even wealthier than they are? Most voting-age-eligible people in our country gave up on voting long ago, and for more than the last half century, our government leaders are elected by a minority of our citizens.

City councils, state legislatures, and Congress go about making laws, being mainly concerned with how they can raise enough money to be re-elected by their minority constituency. Especially at the national level, they have wonderful pensions and medical benefits which virtually no Americans have. Our Congress and President live a life mainly divorced from the public they are supposed to serve. They are clueless about ordinary people's problems.

If the laws of our land represent the will of a minority, and they consistently show disrespect to the highest law of the land, the Constitution, how can our nations truly be a democracy, land of the free? How can we go on a crusade to bring democracy to the world when we are ruled more by—and for—a wealthy minority than by—and for—the people?

PATRIOTISM

Recently, I read a good letter about the meaning of patriotism in your paper. It began by pointing out that love of country is the crucial point, not love of what one's government does.

A deeply caring, respectful and protective attitude toward one's country is at the heart of patriotism, and one may feel this way while despising the policies of government leaders. Indeed, one may feel that government policies are doing great harm to the nation.

A person can be deeply patriotic, yet have despised President Clinton. A person may be deeply patriotic, yet despise President Bush and his regime. Indeed, since most Americans did not vote for George W. Bush in the last election, there was election fraud in Florida, and a conservative, activist Supreme Court awarded the Presidency to Mr. Bush—there is little reason for most Americans to feel respectful toward President Bush.

The backbone of our nation is our Constitution and our traditional ideals of liberty and justice for all. These we must cherish and protect. If some people despise Clinton for being an adulterer and a liar under oath about his cheating ways, that is fine and in no way unpatriotic. If some people despise Bush for being a deceiver and fanatical warmonger, that too is fine and in no way unpatriotic.

Never let Republicans, conservatives or any other political group stake out patriotism as loyalty to them. That is the way of Hitler, fascism or totalitarianism.

STRAIGHT TALK ABOUT SOCIAL SECURITY

Let's talk straight about Social Security and the alleged grave threat to SS. The system is now projected to pay full benefits to all eligible citizens until around 2040. At that point, it will not be bankrupt, but will only be able to pay 70% of the promised benefits to all recipients.

SS is praised as one of the most successful government run programs because it has operated for many decades while allocating little for administrative costs. According to AARP, "Social Security's administrative costs are appreciably lower than the average administrative cost of a mutual fund, which is about 1.5 percent of the account balance."

Right wing extremists have opposed Social Security since its inception. They know it shows government rather than private business can efficiently run a program that benefits the public.

SS is praised because it has successfully helped keep millions of elderly Americans out of poverty in their most vulnerable years. We do need to begin planning about how to keep SS paying full benefits to recipients after 2042, but there is no need to panic and no need to accept President Bush's program for privatizing SS. Remember George W. had poor intelligence about the grave threat Iraq posed to the U.S. Will he do better on this issue?

Privatizing SS, if Bush has his way, will either be done by more massive government borrowing, or the funds SS depends on will become unpredictable and unstable due to not knowing how many younger Americans will choose to use a portion of their SS account for private speculation on the market. Various Wall Street firms are eager to get their hands on new monies to play with on the market.

The alternatives are to raise SS taxes, subsidize the fund with emergency allocations (like we are doing to pay for the war in Iraq and Afghanistan), exclude upper income citizens from SS benefits, reduce benefits, or some combination of the above. I oppose reducing benefits, but the system's projected shortfall 35 years from now can be fixed without following the Bush plan to put more money in the pockets of his rich cronies.

A LIVING WAGE

Those of us in the Green Party favor making the Living Wage a legal requirement for doing business in our community, state, and nation. Congress and our Presidents are slow to raise the minimum wage, a wage insufficient to keep a person above the poverty line, meaning that millions of workers are in jobs where they work for table scraps.

A legally guaranteed Living Wage would mean that all employees would make enough money at their job to live a minimally decent life—having enough to eat, enough for clothes, transportation, and adequate shelter. No matter what kind of job a person has, basic decency requires that the employee earn enough to avoid living in poverty.

The stock argument against this is that it will actually hurt workers because businesses will avoid any areas which require them to pay their employees a Living Wage. No doubt, there is truth in this claim.

Businesses do seek to minimize their costs, and holding down human labor costs is the most convenient way for them to do this. The wider the area (expanding it to the county, state, or nation) covered by Living Wage legislation, the more difficult it will be for business owners to pull up stakes and move elsewhere.

Nevertheless, we need to think long term. We need to let business owners know that we expect them to factor the Living Wage in to their costs of doing business in our community.

Businesses with integrity are not just about the bottom line for the owners, stockholders, and upper-level management staff; they are a team effort (and a social contract) which binds owners, managers, and employees to work together to produce a good or service.

Businesses invariably affect their surrounding communities, and the way they do business is the business of everyone affected. If the owners of a business choose not to operate in a community where they must pay a Living Wage, that is their choice. If they are unwilling care about their community, they should leave it.

"BORROW AND SPEND" REPUBLICANS

It used to be that being Republican meant that a person was fiscally conservative. That was before Ronald Reagan and the Bush dynasty. Now, Republicans feel free to borrow what they cannot pay for now, to run up State and National debt to pay for their visions. The main point is to avoid raising taxes, and even to lower them if possible, while still getting the money to pay for what they want. Another point seems to be to buy votes, hoping to get votes from people who have been spared the pain (in the short term) of paying for government spending.

Imagine what this would mean at a personal level. I want some things, but don't want to spend more of my income to buy them. Instead, I put them on credit so that I will barely feel the cost of what I have bought. When my credit lines are get close to their limit, I simply raise my borrowing limit and continue to buy whatever I want. If things get too bad, and I can no longer use one credit card to pay off another, I declare personal bankruptcy. This would be considered the height of personal irresponsibility, like a child who demands instant gratification but refuses the consequences of his or her behavior.

Done at the political level by "conservatives," does such behavior become mature and acceptable? Let us remember that the Clinton era brought us balanced budgets and budget surpluses while President Reagan and George W. brought us record budget deficits and a growing debt of immense proportions.

Who suffers mainly from the Republican plan to borrow and spend? Middle class, working class, and poor folks suffer. The wealthy don't rely on the government to pay for their kids' education, their health care, or retirement needs. Indeed, members of Congress and the President have wonderful pensions and health care plans, paid for by us. Do you think they will cut those benefits to help pay for our growing national debt? Wall Street's buddy, Alan Greenspan, now recommends Congress reduce the deficit by making cuts in Social Security benefits.

Republicans like to chant that liberals believe in "Tax and Spend" with our money, but Republicans are quite willing to "Borrow and Spend" with our money. Which is more responsible: to raise the money to pay for the government services that most of us need, or to put us in deeper debt while shrinking the services that most of us need?

NEED NATIONAL HEALTH CARE

Tens of millions of Americans are without health care coverage, and many more have substandard coverage. Among the modern, industrialized nations of the West, our nation is alone in having no national health care system. It is shameful and detracts from our nation's claim to greatness.

Recently, our State System of Higher Education forced state university faculty to reduce their health care coverage and to pay more for it. Pennsylvania has for many years ranked toward the bottom of the 50 states in its financial support for education, and the trend continues.

Consider this. Under current insurance coverage offered by the State to university faculty, there is no payment for persons told by their doctor to get a fiberoscopy or colonoscopy to check for cancer of the colon. Early detection of cancer remains the best assurance that it can be successfully treated. Colon cancer is one of the major killers of Americans, and these two procedures are the only methods for checking for polyps in the colon. Our insurance will cover such procedures if there is already evidence of polyps in the colon. What a joke! Still, Blue

Shield has determined that it costs them more to prevent colon cancer than it does to pay for people dying from colon cancer.

We need a national health care system, paid for by citizen dues, otherwise known as taxation. Any Presidential candidate who would pledge a national (affordable) health care system for Americans would likely be elected in a landslide.

THE TRICKLE DOWN THEORY

Remember the "trickle-down theory" popular during Ronald Reagan's reign as President and celebrated even more by the Bush regime? Our Federal government cuts taxes, especially for the wealthy, increases spending and borrowing, runs up record budget deficits and staggering debt—thereby somehow creating milk and honey to flow like rivers through our country.

The theory, very popular among the wealthy and conservatives in our country, holds that the owners of successful corporations and smaller businesses will take their increased revenues (not paid in taxes) to invest in their businesses, create new businesses, and employee more people. This trickle-down may not happen right away, or in the short term, but in the long run, we all are supposed to benefit from the increased wealth of the rich. You have to have faith in the theory in order to give it a chance to work.

Critics, and those of little faith, argue that the theory is a self-serving fantasy which functions to keep the wealthy from facing their own greed and to keep the general public dependent on scraps thrown their way by the corporate elite. Critics argue that the wealthy are just as likely to put their money into bank accounts and other instruments that offer few jobs to few people.

It made me think of another theory, what we might call the "spread-it-around theory" of economics. If we are supposed to accept the trickle-down theory on faith, how about having faith in a different theory of prosperity?

This theory, popular among some economists and appealing to many working class people, holds that the higher the income of most citizens, the more they will spend their money in their communities, thereby spreading prosperity while greasing the consumer-driven economy. Thus, by paying higher wages and salaries to employees, it is supposed that the general welfare of the public is enhanced. Why not pay employees at least a "living wage," enough to keep them out of poverty? Why not give this theory a chance to see if it works?

Critics will argue this theory will undermine our businesses and jobs. Some will say the theory commits the "sin" of socialism or worse.

Which best fits the facts? It is not hard to guess the answer many people will give to this question. Those who benefit most directly from our private enterprise system will defend the first theory, and most of us will be more open to giving the second a try.

KATRINA EXPOSES GOVERNMENT FLAWS

Monster Hurricane Katrina has struck us. New Orleans may be a dead city; tens of thousands of Americans are now refugees in their own country. Oil prices will send the prices of other things spiraling upward.

How will President Bush and Congress be able to cope with this crisis while their war of choice continues to rage in Iraq? Several hundred billion dollars have already gone down that drain.

To finance the war and to give the wealthiest Americans tax cuts, Bush and Congress looted our budget surplus and borrowed us into the oblivion of a huge budget deficit.

How will Bush and Congress find the money and resources to give aid and comfort to the victims of Katrina? Will they have to borrow more and increase our country's titanic debt?

Most of us now will have to learn to live with a lower standard of living. Horrific gas prices and inflation will necessitate we all make do with less.

We have to learn to honor and respect the power of nature, meaning we cannot choose to live in flood zones. Who knows where we will be safe if global warming continues to change ocean currents and brew monster storms?

We need to change our ways of thinking about the world we live in.

We need more conservation, planning, respect for nature, less arrogance in foreign policy, and government officials who understand and respect science.

Most of our leaders, both Democrat and Republican, show no sign they are in touch with the changing world around them.

EARTH DAY

April 22 will be Earth Day, an official day of reverence for Nature celebrated for 35 years. How are we doing? Are we caring, responsible stewards of our planet?

According to 1300 leading scientists from 95 nations, we are doing very poorly and now will have to reap the harvest of our abuse and neglect. Here are some of their conclusions from a report, Millennium Ecosystem Assessment.

Over the past 50 years, humans have changed ecosystems "more rapidly and extensively than at any time in human history." Furthermore, "15 out of 24 ecosystems on Earth have been seriously degraded or used in an unsustainable manner."

Here are a few of the problems. Our population is growing too rapidly. We are releasing too many toxins into the environment (for example, nitrogen and phosphorus in fertilizers), placing huge demands on fresh water sources, causing the extinction of hundreds of species of creatures, and creating climate changes that will be a huge problem for us and a catastrophe for the poor people of the world. We are creating new disease epidemics as human populations huddle together in expanding urban areas, infringe on wilderness areas, and catch exotic viruses.

In general, scientists predict not a total ecosystem collapse on Earth, but the collapse of many local and regional functions. The extent to which global weather patterns will produce global or regional hardships is, of course, hard to predict.

This scientific study is not the report of any environmentalist or "tree hugger" organization, but their conclusions show we humans, and especially those in government, are "fiddling while the planet burns." We need to stop treating the Earth as if it were our toy. We need to make sacrifices, to change our current standard of living. We need to plan long term for the sake of other life and for our own sake. Short term thinking solely in terms of the "bottom line" is infantile and will be our doom.

ODD VOTERS' MINDSET

The areas in our nation most affected by the horror of 9-11 were the District of Columbia, Pennsylvania, and New York (especially New York City). In those areas, nearly 3000 people, most of them U.S. citizens, died as those four planes crashed into buildings and a rural area.

President Bush centered his campaign on reminding us that his main job is to protect Americans and that he was better able to protect us from terrorism than Kerry. Yet, the voters overwhelmingly voted against Bush in the District of Columbia and New York City. They also voted against him statewide in New York and Pennsylvania, although his losing margin was closer in Pennsylvania.

Meanwhile, voters in the most of the Midwest, all of the South, and the Rocky Mountain states (excluding the West Coast) voted for President Bush, overwhelmingly in many of these states. It seems clear that the closer voters were to the tragedies of 9-11, the less they felt Bush was someone who could keep them safe. The further removed Americans were from being affected by 9-11, the more they voted for President Bush.

It is tempting to interpret these results as showing that those Americans who were least threatened by 9-11 terrorism are those who felt the most threatened. In other words, many of the voters in "Red" states seem to be "missing some of their marbles."

BEING CALLED A SOCIALIST

Some weeks ago, Mr. Mehler wrote to you, beginning his letter with "Our socialist friends like Corbin Fowler." I wonder how he would feel if I began this letter by saying "Our neo-Nazi friends like Mr. Mehler." Of course, I would never do such a thing. Tossing around such name-grenades only distracts us from the real issues.

As a Green party member, I think cleaning up our environment should be a high political priority. I also believe the welfare of our community and society trumps the greedy or selfish outlooks of some individuals. While I am not a pacifist, I do favor justice and non-violence as the best way to live our lives, and I think the use of violence by our government should always be a method of last resort. If that makes me a "socialist" according to some ill-informed points of view, I am happy to be so labeled.

In order to keep our freedom, we must be vigilant and brave enough to resist our own government when officials engage in propaganda and a reckless disregard for our citizen's Constitutional rights. Our President is not courageous, but reckless in his "Bring it on" war policies. He risks nothing, but asks others to risk everything.

Our nation did a good thing by eventually deciding to resist and help defeat Hitler. We can be proud of that. That was 60 years ago. Not every foreign leader who opposes U.S. foreign policy is a Hitler or madman. Some people need to stay informed about the present and stop living in a distant past.

Clinton's lies about oral sex undermined his marriage vows while Bush regime lies have cost tens of thousands of lives. 19 terrorists, almost all from Saudi Arabia, devastated buildings, planes, and lives in NYC, D.C. and rural Pennsylvania. Bush responded by devastating most of Iraq, a nation which had nothing to do with the 9-11 attacks. Prior to the Bush invasion, Iraq was not a breeding ground for terrorism, but our CIA says the invasion has made Iraq a training ground for terrorism against the West.

I love and honor my country by opposing the reckless and criminal behavior of "leaders" like President Bush. People like Bush, Rice, Gonzales, Ashcroft, Cheney, and Rumsfeld bring shame to our nation. Some of them should be impeached (according to former U.S. Attorney General, Ramsey Clark), and some should be on trial for war crimes.

TWILIGHT ZONE POLITICS

The most recent Gallup Poll finds that President Bush has the lowest second term approval rating of any President since World

War 2, the lowest in 60 years. 45% approve of his job performance and 49% disapprove. His approval ratings are lower than Clinton's, Nixon's, and Johnson's—all men who also had trouble telling the truth.

What a world we live in! George W. Bush is now less approved of than Presidents who lied about their adulterous affairs, war and peace, burglary, and setting up secret police squads answering only to the White House. Yet, when elected by a slim margin in 2004 for his first term as our elected President, George W. claimed he had a mandate to spend his accumulated political capital.

How odd to be the citizen of a great democracy where most people choose not to vote, where a President can be selected for office when not winning a majority of the vote! How odd that a man can be praised for his courageous leadership in a war he himself does not fight and when, as a young man, he evaded another war and much of his National Guard service!

How odd that a man who underachieved or failed at everything until he got elected Governor of Texas can be viewed as Time's Man of the Year last year! How odd that a silver spoon-fed, rich boy can be viewed by so many working class men as an ordinary guy just like them! How strange that this man can tell Syria they must withdraw their occupying forces from

Lebanon, that they must stop meddling in another nation's affairs while that same man orders his own troops to invade and occupy Iraq!

Sometimes, it feels like I have stepped into the Twilight Zone or Through the Looking Glass. A country ruled by the people and for the people is a beautiful idea! I hope we get a country like that some day.

BEING LIBERAL IS GOOD

For decades now, conservatives have used the word `liberal' as a weapon, and national Democrats have denied that they are liberals. Politicians are afraid that if people know they are liberals, they won't get elected or re-elected. They are afraid they will be associated in "the pubic mind" with some kind extremism. Conservatives, on the other hand, don't run from being called `conservative' even though there are right wing extremists with whom they could be associated.

The terms of this silly and dangerous word game have been defined by clever conservatives, but the truth has been a casualty. How does Webster's New World Dictionary (1984) define `liberal'? Liberal is defined as 1. generous, 2. ample or abundant, 3. not literal or strict, 4. tolerant or broadminded, 5. favoring reform or progress.

Some religious conservatives probably do not like any attitude that they deem "not strict" or "tolerant," but do mainstream Americans dislike and distrust generosity, abundance, or a commitment to reform and progress? Give me a break. This is ridiculous.

Democrats became a political power by favoring reform and progress and by advocating generosity and abundance. Does anyone remember FDR and the New Deal or LBJ and the War on Poverty? Indeed, long ago, Republicans under Abraham Lincoln were liberals on the issue of abolishing slavery in our country. Liberals should be very proud of being liberal.

Because national Democrats have run away from being called "liberals," they are cowardly. Democrats try to look like Republicans. This strategy worked for Clinton, but he had lots of personal charisma and still got far less than 50% of the vote in 1992. In the meanwhile, the wealthy have always played "the class card", getting richer while more of us get poorer.

Democrats have allowed neoconservatives to define who they are. Voters see little difference between Republican candidates and Democrats, so they naturally vote for the candidates they feel are the most sincere about the values they express, namely the Republicans.

LIBERAL VERSUS CONSERVATIVE

The worldviews of conservatives and liberals are so very different that it is nearly impossible to settle their differences by appeal to the facts. The problem is that they don't agree on what the facts are or even the standards for determining the facts.

Modern conservatives take it as self-evident that the less government we have, the better off we are—with two notable exceptions. They want to invest huge sums in the military, and they want to subsidize the operations of U.S. business interests. They take it as self-evident that government operations are always less efficient than those run by private enterprise. They are convinced that domestic welfare programs will be abused, and hence, we should cut back welfare.

On the other hand, liberals take it as self-evident that the purpose of government is to provide services for the public. They assume that big government is bad only to the extent that it is not using tax money to provide needed services for the public. Liberals do not think it is necessarily wise to spend huge sums of tax dollars on the military or to promote U.S. business interests. They fear the abuses and waste of corporate welfare.

Some conservatives like to say that liberals are eager to "blame America first" for world problems and to see our government's actions in foreign policy as the cause of evil around the globe. Conservatives tend to blame everyone else first before accepting US blame for international predicaments. They are like children who refuse to take any personal responsibility for creating problems in their life. If liberals are mired in guilt, conservatives are mired in denial.

About the Author

Corbin Fowler is a tenured professor of philosophy at Edinboro University of Pennsylvania. He grew up in Cheyenne, Wyoming, received a B.A. in philosophy from the University of Wyoming, and a Ph.D. in philosophy from the University of Nebraska. He was a campus leader during the student power and ant-war movements of the late 60s and early 70s. During graduate school in Lincoln, Nebraska, he worked to impeach Richard Nixon for Nixon's various crimes and violations of the *Constitution*. While teaching at Central Missouri State University and the University of Wisconsin-Oshkosh (1979-1986), he founded two local peace-with-justice groups.During his academic career, Dr. Fowler has taught at public and private universities and colleges, from

Wyoming to Pennsylvania and from Wisconsin to Kentucky. He has given numerous professional presentations at conferences in the United Sates and some in Europe. He is also the author of many professional articles and two books: *The "Logic" of U.S. Weapons' Policy* (1987) and *Morality for Moderns* (1996). He is the managing editor and cofounder (1998) of *Janua Sophia*, an undergraduate journal of philosophy. His current teaching interest is how we can understand ourselves better by examining public and private myth.

He met his wife Patti Repko while both were working to protest the first Gulf War in the early 90s. Patti and Corbin live in Edinboro, Pennsylvania with their son, Corbin Sterling Fowler, and their wonderful cat, Charlotte.

CWG Press is owned and operated by Chuck Gregory in Fort Lauderdale, FL. Rather than limiting our books to a specific genre, we look for books that are of good quality. We choose our authors and our books carefully, and we are proud of them.